The Talking Stick
Volume Twenty One
Nightfall

The Talking Stick
Volume Twenty One
Nightfall

A publication of the
Jackpine Writers' Bloc

Published by the Jackpine Writers' Bloc, Inc.
Send correspondence to Jackpine Writers' Bloc,
13320 149th Ave, Menahga, Minnesota 56464.
sharrick1@wcta.net

*This activity is made possible, in part, by a grant provided by
the Region 2 Arts Council through funding from the Minnesota
State Legislature.*

ISBN: 978-1-928690-21-4

Table of Contents

Poetry, Creative Nonfiction and Fiction

Table of Contents

Poetry, Creative Nonfiction and Fiction

Table of Contents
Poetry, Creative Nonfiction and Fiction

Table of Contents

Poetry, Creative Nonfiction and Fiction

Co-Editor's Note

Sharon Harris
Editor's Choice: "Ghost Writing" by Kevin Zepper (p. 51)

My favorite poem this year is "Ghost Writing." I have never tried Prose Poetry, but this writer is exceptional at it. The poem is imaginative; the poet did something with a subject that I would not have thought of doing. Such a clever play on words. A ghost writer does the writing behind the scenes for other authors, helping them with their writing. In this poem, we see spectral ink, otherworldly words appearing, free-floating ideas, all actually coming from ghosts as words manifest on any stray piece of paper. Very clever.

Several days ago, this line kept popping into my head: Alone on the Earth. That is how I was feeling. The weather was gray and damp and dismal and desolate. On low days like this, I feel like I have absolutely no one to confide in or talk to, no one I can connect to. Clearly, I spend too much time alone. Everyone is too busy, too involved in their own lives. I am just a bother and an interruption—as I suppose sometimes they are to me. Most days, I feel like I am surrounded and crowded by people and their noise, but they are really so distant from me. I have no connection to them.

Each of us sometimes feels that yawning depth inside us. That emptiness. That need to be filled and held and needed and noticed and appreciated. Loved. That's what it really is, isn't it?

Or am I feeling this way because I just turned sixty? Perhaps. And is that why I write? To try to reach people? To connect with someone—anyone—to erase that loneliness, even for just a moment? I believe it is. I need—we all need—to feel a connection to other souls. We need to know that others have felt what we are feeling—that there are many things that make our life experiences similar. We need to know that we are not alone on the earth.

x

Co-Editor's Note

Tarah L. Wolff
Editor's Choice: "Censored" by Joanne Moren (p. 81)

We read to realize (after page three hundred and twelve maybe. . .) that we started a book a few hours ago. We certainly did not begin our love affair with words with text books or text messages. I began my own reading addiction with a book that took me so far away, so immediately and so entirely, that I could never imagine a world without books again. It is for this reason that I chose Joanne Moren's poem (Censored, p. 81) for my Editor's Choice this year. I chose it because until the very last line I forget that I am reading, or that a writer is dictating my experience at all. I can see the lovers, feel the rug beneath me, hear the crackling fire, and know what it is like to be completely nude with another, and face no judgment. It is only in the capture of the last line when I realize that I have been led. I am not in a room, nor am I peeking in a window; I am reading.

What impresses me so much about poetry is that it is capable of transporting us just as completely (and sometimes far more quickly) as any novel. It only takes a few words (the right words) and we are enthralled.

This is the twenty-first Talking Stick. Amazing. I have been a member of Jackpine and a part of this book longer than I can believe. I have lost beloved pets, seen divorces, seen the other kids in my family have kids of their own (even though we were never supposed to grow up) and driven thousands of miles since I became a part of all of this. And now I have even seen my own first novel finished (or, as maybe most writers would agree: I just had to stop myself at some point) and in print and for sale on Amazon.com. Something I do not believe would ever have come to pass without this group or without this book.

This is the twenty-first edition of the Talking Stick and, if I could, I would take this little book out for her first drink. I certainly think she deserves it!

The Judges

Poetry Judge:

LouAnn Shepard Muhm

LouAnn Shepard Muhm lives in northern Minnesota where she writes and teaches. Her poems have appeared in various literary journals, as well as in several anthologies. She was a finalist for the Creekwalker Poetry Prize and the Late Blooms Postcard Series, both in 2007. LouAnn received the Minnesota State Arts Board Artist Initiative Grant in Poetry in 2006 and 2012. Her poetry collection *Breaking the Glass* (2008, Loonfeather Press) was a finalist for the Midwest Book Award in Poetry.

Creative Nonfiction Judge:

Susan Hauser

Susan Carol Hauser is an essayist, poet and natural history writer. Her most recent book is *My Kind of River Journey: Seeking Passage on the Mississippi*. She received a 2011-2012 MSAB Artist's Initiative Grant and a 2010-2011 McKnight Artist Fellowship Loft Award in Poetry.

Fiction Judge:

Candace Simar

Candace Simar is a writer and poet from Pequot Lakes, Minnesota. Publishing her Minnesota-based historical novels about Scandinavian immigrants during the 1862 Dakota Conflict, *Abercrombie Trail* in 2009, *Pomme De Terre* in 2010 and *Birdie* in 2011, has been a dream come true. Candace is a grateful recipient of Five Wings Art Grants funded in part by the McKnight Foundation. Her next book, *Blooming Prairie,* will be released in the fall of 2012.

Poetry

First Place $300: "Truck Stop"
Mike Finley (p. 1)

Mike Finley has lived in Minnesota for most of the last forty years. He is a poet, journalist, videographer, and essayist. In 2011, his collected works *Yukon Gold* was published by Kraken Press. He is a 1985 winner of the Pushcart Prize. In 1995, his book *Why Teams Don't Work* was named "Best Book, The Americas" by *The Financial Times*.

Creative Nonfiction

First Place $300: "Crisscross"
Cindy Fox (p. 2)

Cindy Fox grew up on a dairy farm near New York Mills, Minnesota. After forty years in the Twin Cities, she retired in 2007 from her job as an Export Import Compliance Manager. She now lives at the end of a dead-end road near Shevlin, Minnesota, where she has found an ideal place to write. Cindy has contributed stories to *Farm & Ranch Living, Steam Traction, Area Journeys, Northwoods Woman, The Talking Stick,* and *20x20 Art & Words.*

Fiction

First Place $300: "Perfect is as Perfect Does"
Sandra Clough (p. 3)

In 2001, Sandra Clough left a corporate job of twenty-five years and discovered the joy of creative writing. Since that time, her work has been published in *Cricket Magazine* (for children ages nine to fourteen) and *Talking Stick* Volumes 17, 19, and 20. She resides in Burnsville, Minnesota.

Poetry

Second Place $100
"Patriarch" by Betty J. Benner (p. 6)

Honorable Mention
"After the Funeral" by Marlene Mattila Stoehr (p. 47)
"The Immigrant, 1906" by Peggy Trojan (p. 191)
"Sock Drawer" by Sue Reed Crouse (p. 88)
"Down There" by Laura L. Hansen (p. 98)

Creative Nonfiction

Second Place $100
"Saying Goodbye to Dad" by Janet Preus (p. 7)

Honorable Mention
"Dear Military Service Member" by Emily Brisse (p. 189)
"First Apartment" by Louise Bottrell (p. 171)
"Knots" by Jean Childers (p. 23)

Fiction

Second Place $100
"Bologna Sandwich" by D. A. Berg (p. 10)

Honorable Mention
"Long Winter" by Dennis Herschbach (p. 65)

The Talking Stick
Volume Twenty-One
Nightfall

Truck Stop

The older man in the leather vest
Walks with the gait of a gunfighter
Toward the men's room, a gallon bottle
Of pink windshield wash
In one hand and a bag full of cigarettes
And Hostess Sno Balls in the other.
He is compact and erect, and his mustache
Is trim despite hours on the road.
His white-haired woman, taking smaller steps,
Follows close behind, eyebrows penciled
In an "I will follow you anywhere" arc,
Her frame a little dumpy from the miles
She has kept his company, but you can see
There was a time when she was wonderful.
Is he a good man? I can't tell. But I admire
The seriousness he girds himself in.
Like the last sworn knight in a useless world
Ambling past the Sega Strike Fighter
And the "For Your Safety" condom dispensary,
Past the claw-fetching crane game and the
Lip-biting girl eying the Tickle Me Elmo
Embedded in the heap.

1

Crisscross

I sit in the front pew reserved for the family and stare at the American flag draped over my father's casket. I think to myself, *I'm glad he is covered. He was always so cold.*

The stripes are blurry like ripples on a pond and, each time I blink, they spread and intersect with the stars in endless combinations. While the minister recites Psalm 23, images bubble to the surface of my muddled mind. I see my father, a lifelong farmer, lying in green pastures. For a moment, my grief subsides and I think how happy he must be there and, even more, when Mother met him at the gate. After the final *Amen*, I keep my head down and listen to the church turn deathly quiet.

The silence is penetrated by the sharp ring of gunshots splitting me wide open. I rise and lay my hand over my chest to somehow stop the bleeding. More gunshots fire off in unison, a final salute to honor my father's service in the military. When the mournful bugle rings in the cold, crisp air, it taps into my heart and sucks me dry.

Members of the local VFW Post walk like toy soldiers up to his casket. Faces stoic, they fold the flag into a triangle—crisscross, crisscross, crisscross—until the stripes are tucked under the stars. A former classmate of mine, a Vietnam Vet, turns and presents the flag to me—the next of kin.

I stretch out my arms, palms facing upwards, and he respectfully lays it there for me to honor and cherish. He salutes me and my body trembles as I stare once again at the flag that was draped over my father's casket—all tucked in—and I feel so cold.

Perfect Is As Perfect Does

When I told the gals at work that Hank and I were coming to Victor's Trattoria, they were agog. "It's so exclusive," they said, "and so expensive."

"What will you wear?"

I didn't run out and buy a new outfit because I'm not here by choice. I'd just as soon be at Olive Garden having their Three Cheese Lasagna and a glass of the house red, but a couple years ago, my baby sister married a rich guy and now she gives me gift certificates to places like this for my birthday. (I still give her bath salts I buy at Sears with my employee discount, but that's another story.)

It's hard to relax at Victor's. The waiters hover and call everyone *madam* and *sir*. They won't let you put your napkin on your lap by yourself and, should you drop bread crumbs on their snowy tablecloths—or heaven forbid—dribble wine, they're right there to clean up after you. I can't pronounce anything on the menu and the only thing that costs under $50 is a meatless entree made of vegetables I've never heard of.

It's not hard to spot the regulars. The men wear suits and ties and starched shirts and look like they're straight out of the boardroom. The women all look like they spent the day at a spa, getting facials and manicures.

Hank and I've been seated at a table in the corner—so as not to be too big a blemish on all this perfection, I suspect. Hank doesn't care that we're hopelessly out of place. He has his head buried in the menu, so I peruse the wine list. A pricey Chardonnay catches my eye. "Citrus overtones balanced on an underpinning of oak." I don't know about overtones and underpinnings, but it sounds tasty and I look around for the waiter.

He, of course, is busy fussing over an especially perfect-looking couple nearby. Obviously, regulars. He even calls them by name—Mr. and Mrs. Peterman. After taking their complicated drink orders, he practically genuflects as he backs away before scurrying off. Certainly, no time to stop by our table. Hank is salivating over the entree listings, so I let my gaze linger on the Petermans.

Truthfully, I can hardly take my eyes off them, especially Mrs. Peterman. Her ash-blond hair is chin length and somehow looks simple and elegant at the same time. Her dress is probably cashmere. A shade darker than her hair, it clings to her perfectly proportioned figure, making me painfully aware of my outdated pantsuit bought four years and ten pounds ago.

Mrs. Peterman is one of those women who make women like me wish we'd finished our college degrees and joined a health club. When she and her husband were being seated and the waiter floated a napkin onto her lap, she smiled up at him with just the right combination of warmth and aloofness. When he did the same for me, I giggled like a school girl and snatched it out of his hands.

Good Lord! He's back with their drinks already. Perhaps now he'll check in with us.

But alas, no hovering here. Not only are we *not* a blemish, we are invisible.

The Petermans pause their conversation long enough to sip their drinks. They've been quite engrossed in each other. Probably discussing a play they saw last night or where to spend their next vacation.

Full disclosure: I'm jealous. Now that our kids are out of the house, I worry that Hank and I have nothing left in common. Whenever we talk anymore, we argue. Hank's keeping his head in the menu right now because he's miffed that I made an appointment for us to look into long-term health care insurance. He says I dwell on getting old. I say I like to plan ahead.

I can't picture the Petermans arguing over anything, let alone insurance. I'm sure their golden years are *nicely* taken care of.

Hank's phone buzzes. He digs it out of his pocket and answers quietly, then says to hold on. It's work, he tells me, and slips away from the table to find a place to talk.

Since there's no wine on the horizon and all this blinding perfection is giving me a headache, I look around for the restroom. Skirting the Petermans' table, I see that Mrs. Peterman's skin is flawless, her manicure looks fresh, and the diamond on her left hand is the size of a walnut.

Down a short hallway, I locate the ladies' room. Closing the door on the bustle and hum of the dining room, I feel as though I've stepped into yet another world. A golden glow emanates from ornate sconces flanking the mirrors above the

4

basins and a vaguely familiar jazz melody wafts from hidden speakers. After a few bars, I realize it's a song Hank and I were crazy about in college but, try as I might, I'm unable to recall the group. Somebody's Trio. Hank will remember. Since I'm the only one in the bathroom, I sit down on a small, velvet-covered bench and close my eyes. The wail of the sax begins to paint a picture. Hank's college apartment. A flickering candle jammed in the top of a Chianti bottle we'd just emptied. Me, wrapped in Hank's arms swaying to this song.

Just as the music ends, the bathroom door opens, admitting one of Victor's Perfect Patrons. She throws me a glance on her way into a stall, but doesn't acknowledge me. She probably thinks I'm the attendant and for some reason this makes me giggle.

Heading back to the dining room, still smiling and that wonderful song still in my head, I'm stopped short by a resounding crash, followed by an eerie silence. No more clink of cutlery, no more buzz of conversation. Just silence. As I round the corner, I see why.

The Petermans' table has been upended. At first glance, I think a leg broke, perhaps due to a manufacturing flaw. Then I see the martini glass dangling from Mrs. Peterman's fingers and the remains of her martini running down Mr. Peterman's face. Her perfect features contort as she screeches names at him I've only heard said aloud in R-rated movies. Now she's shouting that she's known for years he was cheating and, if he thought he could tell her he's divorcing her here at Victor's so she wouldn't make a scene, he's got another think coming. And just to be sure he's gotten the point, she hurls her glass at the wall.

A half-dozen waiters descend on the pair while their fellow diners look on in disbelief. And no wonder—this bubble of perfection just burst.

A guilty glee overtakes me as I stride toward the door in search of Hank. I'm dying to tell him what he missed . . . and about the woman thinking I was a maid . . . and to ask him about the song.

Maybe we'll hash it all over at Olive Garden, with Three Cheese Lasagna and a glass of the house red.

Patriarch

He rules the family
with the razor strap hanging by the back door,
with the cross tattooed on his left hand
that moves every which way
as his fist makes his point.
We are hooked.

It is the culture
which says fathers are to be obeyed, regardless.

It is the mother, his wife,
who suffers,
passes her woes on to the children.

Patriarch.
He is the story of the earth,
the myth that says strength and thrust
make the world go 'round,
the myth that says the world grows
out of woman crushed
and that every family needs
a razor strap at the back door.

Saying Goodbye to Dad

At some point, perhaps on Highway 87 between Perham and Wolf Lake, I must have realized that I was saying goodbye to Dad because I was writing a song about it. I had a chorus at this point and I sang it over and over again:

"I'm saying goodbye to Dad, enjoying all we have . . ."

Then verse after verse poured out of me—about his hunting and fishing, mystery novels, crossword puzzles, rare roast beef, freezing green beans, *Reader's Digest* jokes—detail after detail. Just me and the words, keeping each other company on my weekend drive to and from the lake where Mom and Dad had retired a generation ago.

I always seemed to be driving with a dazzling sunset and glowing fall colors too beautiful for words, but the imperfect words about Dad kept coming:

"He said, 'I think I'll live forever,'
And we all thought he would,
But at ninety he's finally getting old."

Those, and dozens more lines, never made it into the final version of the song:

"His collar's loose around his neck
He used to be so tall . . ."

No. There's nothing pathetic about him—not with his dancing blue eyes and resonant voice calling "Somebody!" from the bedroom. He always said, "Thank you very much," when we moved the pillows or found his magazine, which had slipped between the bed and the wall.

"We work a crossword puzzle; he's faster than I am.
Soon he's sleeping in his favorite chair."

I had to keep the line for the lines that followed, although my dad deserved better prosody.

"Glasses on his nose, the pencil in his hand,

How will I find the words when he's not there?"

Really, that's pretty bad, the accent on "will." For Dad, it should have been perfect. It is technical details like this that keep me focused on the song and on the road. More than once, my face awash in tears, I pull over and hunt for fast food napkins. The tissues are long gone.

And there are way too many details; the song is much too dense. I know I can't cram my lifetime with him into one song anyway, but how will I decide? Surely, out of all these details I can rhyme perfectly good ones *and* get the prosody. And so it goes . . . arguments with my technical songwriter, who keeps me on the road.

"I drape another blanket 'cross his knees."

I've never draped a blanket 'cross his knees. Is that dishonest? It is a song after all, not a documentary. He *did* say something about "don't let Mama's flowers freeze." The obvious rhymes were way too obvious. Or sneeze? He always said he was allergic to dust and wore a bandana over his face when we swept the garage. Anyway, not "sneeze." Another twenty miles or so of self-dialogue. The sun has set and the sky is pink, mauve, melon, and—what is that color? Blaze orange, I guess, like his deer hunting coat.

"What a privilege to care for him.
And ease the worry on his face."

Now just wait a minute. Did I really ease any worry on his face? More like he eased the worry on my face. But the little bit of "What a Friend We Have in Jesus" melody is cool. The rest of that bridge:

"Every thought becomes a prayer for him;
He's leaving with such grace."

I once wrote *"there's farewell on his face."* Bad. Not only was it not true, it was a stupid line. I really feel better when I recognize stupid lines and laugh at myself for having ever written them down. I never cry when I am dealing with stupid lines. *"He's leaving with such grace"* makes me cry.

I suppose he didn't see it that way. He looked at me once and said, "I'm just falling apart." I said, "Yeah, I guess you are." There was no denying it. He was perfectly lucid and we both knew his body was leaving faster than the rest of him wanted to go. Not too long after that, the rest of him seemed to be tentatively exploring his new home. Sometimes I, too, felt a detachment from this earth:

"His angel wings already show—
A glimpse of heaven, oh, I know
He's more prepared than me for letting go!"

Was he? I am past Perham and in more traffic. I resent the invasion into my floating, private world. Am I grieving already? I hadn't put that name to it.

"I know I'm lucky I've got time . . ."

But it's never enough time. We didn't go fishing again, or pick raspberries or haul brush. I never helped you clean out the basement, Dad. Not that you cared; it was for Mom. How about all those cigar boxes full of bolts, screws, washers and—what are those things, anyway?

"Enjoying all we have . . ."

Well, never mind. My trips through the core of Minnesota's lake country will have a newly defined mission from this point. We are gathered, my five siblings and I, with Mom, whose fingers lightly fidget with Dad's pajama top. No one knows about the song that has prepared me for this moment; someone starts, "My faith looks up to Thee . . ." By the time we are halfway through verse two, which only some of us remember, we know we wouldn't have to finish, but we do.

Fiction - D. A. Berg

Second Place

Bologna Sandwich

Death is typically the end to a long marriage. For Gertrude and Harry, it was a bologna sandwich. Harry lives in my basement now, two doors down from Gertrude's house. You would think after fifty-one years of marriage, Gertrude would have known that Harry likes hard-salami, not bologna. Anyway, bologna was the straw that broke the camel's back. I believe it was an old weary camel, with a multitude of straws, before Gertrude slipped Oscar Mayer's finest in front of Harry.

Years ago, we'd hang out in our back yards and grill. Our kids would play games and get grass stains on their clothes. With tongs and beer in hand, Harry and I would talk about the Minnesota Twins, fishing and hunting. Gertrude and my wife Mary, God rest her soul, would sit at the picnic table, drink iced-tea, eat chips and dip, and talk about the kids, removing grass stains, and all that woman stuff. Harry and I hunted, fished, and golfed too, but not very often, as Gertrude had an endless list of reasons Harry needed to stay home.

Us neighbor guys worked on projects. We might paint a garage one week, put up a fence the next, or fix a car on a weeknight. There was always something to work on and we enjoyed the camaraderie. Harry has always been one of those guys willing to lend a hand, at least when Gertrude would let him, which was usually the week before they had a project to do, and a few days after it was done.

Within fifteen minutes of being served the bologna sandwich, Harry showed up with a grocery bag full of clothes, his fishing gear, and his golf clubs slung over his shoulder. "Can I stay with you for a while, Kal?"

"Sure," I said.

Once I found out what was going on, I encouraged reconciliation.

"If she hasn't changed after all these years, why should I expect her to change now?"

"What about counseling?"

"Doesn't work. Tried it four times. She's got no respect for the counselors and no respect for me."

His children came to talk sense into him, one at a time at first, including one who flew in from Oregon, and another who drove non-stop from Indiana. This did no good. Then all five showed up together. I was in the garage sharpening my lawnmower blade. The kitchen window was open because I had burned Spam that morning. My garage is close to the kitchen window. After some discussion, Harry slammed his coffee cup on the table and let loose. "Your mother does not respect me! All those years, she pushed me around. Telling me what I could and couldn't do. She'd throw tantrums if she didn't get her way. I let her do it to protect you all from her tirades. By the time you all grew up and moved out, I had pretty much given up. I don't know why I waited so long, but I've had enough!"

They gave up shortly after he pointed out that two of them were divorced. Later, I guided the conversation in a way in which he would not realize I may have overheard bits and pieces of the conversation and never got the lawnmower blade sharpened, to find out what triggered his behavior.

"Well," Harry said. "We watched this movie *About Schmidt* with Jack Nicholson. His wife had made him sit down on the toilet whenever he took a leak, and after she died he rebelled by standing up to pee, and then he commenced to piss all over the bathroom floor. He let it rip! Got it out of his system! I thought it was funny as hell, but Gertrude sat there clicking her knitting needles in disgust. I got to thinking: it's not often a husband lives longer than his wife, and I have high blood pressure. The next day at lunch, she serves up bologna. It was more than I could take. You know the rest."

I went to the lawyer's office with Harry. He must have wanted backup, I guess. Anyway, he tells the lawyer he wants to divorce for irreconcilable differences. He goes on to tell about that movie called *The Great Outdoors* with John Candy and Dan Aykroyd. "Well, that Dan Aykroyd character tells John Candy that hotdogs are made of lips and assholes. What is bologna but a hot dog in sandwich meat form, and what could be more irreconcilable than serving someone lips and assholes for lunch?"

I wondered to myself if hard-salami wasn't made with lips and assholes too, but didn't pose the question. Anyway, the lawyer could read between the slices of bread and empathized with Harry, but refrained from using that analogy in the proceedings. Four months after Harry showed up at my door, and nearly fifty-two years after he walked down the aisle, he was a free man again.

Gertrude got the house and most of Harry's retirement funds. Harry and I came to rental terms. Harry needed extra income and got a job as a greeter at Walmart where he is frequently complimented for his smile. I was bored and took a job there, too. We work the same shift, four days a week.

We began taking morning walks five days a week and worked up to five miles. Harry suggested we jog a mile of that. So we upgraded from sneakers to running shoes. We golf three or four days a week and bowl in the winter. We help the younger guys in the neighborhood remodel work we did years ago. We look and feel dang good for a couple of guys in their mid-seventies. Harry's blood pressure has dropped and he uses less medication.

Once during a snow storm, we were playing cribbage and drinking a few beers. We went out to the backyard to check things out. One thing led to another and before we knew it, we two old farts, standing in a blizzard with beers in hand, were having a pissing contest. Literally! We had streams out nearly two feet. We couldn't tell who pissed the farthest on account of the wind, but it felt good to have some pressure—the fruits of all that exercise to be sure. Thankfully that is the only abnormal pissing Harry has done at my house. I've been worried he might pull an *About Schmidt*.

It's been hard on Gertrude. She peeks out when Harry and I go by. She hangs out at the Senior Center on the prowl for a new husband; no luck so far. I feel sorry for her, but she pushed Harry around for all those years and never said she was sorry or offered to change. Harry never looks at the house, ever.

We've settled into a routine and things are going well for us. We are enjoying retirement to the fullest. We are planning on renting an RV this summer and this odd couple will explore the American West.

One peculiar thing though: ever since the divorce was finalized, every day, without fail, Harry makes himself a bologna sandwich for lunch.

Vanishing Act

After the denouement of
fifteen years of marriage

I watch evidence
existential
in letters
and cards
slowly disappearing

saying "I love you"

saying "I love"

saying "I"

Unspoken Words

Broken, red-cased travel alarm
received for my twelfth Christmas;
black clutch purse with broken zipper
my dad gave me for my birthday.

It's strange the meaning you
attach to a gift: some brass gears,
red vinyl and a white clock face.
A symbol of passage,
of childhood completed.

Golden monogram on
that old clutch purse sang
the song of a father's love,
words of the heart
held in pieces of plastic.

These, along with other mementos,
were placed in the first of many knapsacks,
cradles of treasured memories,
carried down the road.

Fiction - Sarah Lorraine Chick Tyler
Weak Aching Hearts

We cut through the haze of the early morning, Janice, Marty, the Preacher, and I. Stumbling our way down to the breakers, tripping in the deep sand. Almost all of us are wearing inappropriate shoes. We are unprepared for the long walk down the beach and for what we have come to do. We are unprepared for the angry sea that greets us. It spills over the jetty and onto the coast, greedy and anxious, as if it knows what we have brought and doesn't want to wait for us to hand it over.

The last time I spoke to Marty was over the phone. She was raving, the junk raging through her veins.

"I've been standing on one leg for three damn years, waiting for God to do me a favor."

My words could not reach her. Much like the violence that is implicit when sleeping with a knife under one's pillow, Marty had become something entirely cold and strange.

I pass out flowers. Carnations, hideously, artificially colored carnations. A Technicolor nightmare. They remind me of the nightmares where I see her face. Tramadol-flavored fever dreams in which I scream and scream until she turns to me and says, "You look so surprised. Stop it. You know damn well this is the life we chose."

The Preacher begins his sermon, Ave Maria or some such. Whatever salve men of the cloth slather on weak, aching hearts. The sign of the cross is completed and I stand back and watch as the three of them approach the sea.

Janice and the Preacher have their hands full. Padre is clutching his bible in one hand and Janice's belt loop in the other. He holds on tight as she leans over the edge of the abyss. And Janice, poor Jan, holds the turquoise urn that contains the earthly remains of her sister. A black cassock flapping in the wind, a flash of turquoise, and she is gone.

15

My sweet Martina, my love, I want to follow you. I want to ride with you on a cloud of manic indulgence until there is no more sky. But you are gone. Gone, down to that world of drowned sailors, the ashes of former human beings, and the broken hearts of those left standing on the shore. So it goes. Organic matter given over to decay, the beautiful human form, the spoils of nothing.

We turn our backs on it. We throw our flowers into the ocean and begin to leave it all behind. As we walk, dots of blue, fuchsia, and neon yellow catch my eye. The carnations. Apparently the ocean has seen enough ugliness for one day and can stomach no more.

"Amen to that," I think, and start the fumbling, silent, stupid walk toward the rest of my days.

Same Old Story

I see sadness outside the window of
this coffee shop. The man and woman
stand apart. His gestures are vivid with
disgust. Words I cannot hear, flow from
a mouth drawn and angry.

Her face I cannot see. She moves
little. Her body is quiet.
I know its sadness and am sorry, yet
glad to not know the story.

Bucky

He never made a fuss
about his aching hips
or his crushing tumors,

Never whined when
he couldn't run with the others
or needed her help up the stairs.

He never refused his food,
just wagged and smiled
with that giant tongue,

Slipped away one morning
before she was up,
not wanting to cause a fuss.

The Dig

Inside the cemetery gate, crowded minivans arrive, scattering dust from the gravel road. I stand next to Dylan —what's left of his body, four pounds of ash in an urn, super-glued shut. *Lean into the grief,* they say. I don't just lean into the grief, I dig into it. Each time I go under, I never come out the same. And every time I think I've just about got grief figured out, she comes back like a Mourning Dove, nesting near a grave.

I don't want to be here. I don't want to relive Dylan's death. I don't want to be reminded how my nephew went out to get the mail and never came back; how Shelley found him in the ditch struck by a feed truck, gave him CPR and said, "After a while you don't taste the blood."

Two months ago, Shelley sat around Dylan's hospital room asking a chaplain, *When does the soul leave the body, when the heart dies, or the brain?* She could have held on to her thirteen-year-old son's body, wearing SpongeBob boxers, and newly developed abs. Not a scratch on him from the neck down. I tell you, he looked angelic, asleep in a white turban—not a kid in a coma with bandages covering his shattered skull. Yet, when I opened his eyelids, his green eyes were no longer vibrant; his pupils sat fixed and vacant. My sister told him, "Go to God. Mommy's going to be okay."

He died five minutes later.

Wearing a floral dress, the breeze lightly lifting the hem of her skirt, Shelley stands in the center of the cemetery, hugging and talking to people like we're at a family picnic. She's the happiest I've seen her in weeks. I realize, for her this day is no harder than any other day. All the days since Dylan died.

My kids go up and hug her. We used to joke about the irony: how she wanted a litter of kids, struggled to conceive, and was blessed with Dylan. While I, on the other hand, never really planned on having kids and got pregnant with the third on "The Pill."

We gather around Dylan's marker. The pastor starts quoting scripture. I get lost in the liturgy and look toward my mother. She bought this stone—the last gift she will buy Dylan. She came out to the cemetery yesterday and was very upset: "If someone sits on that bench, their nasty feet will touch Dylan's headstone."

Dug-up grass has been patted down; the marker has been moved. My mother can be quite persuasive in matters such as this. She is the stone keeper, the grave keeper, the curator of grass—adding her touch of beauty above the bones. She's been known to drive around the countryside to tend to grave sites, planting flowers for her loved ones. Sixty-two and widowed twice, once from suicide, once from cancer. Divorced from my father, she said: "Wouldn't you know—he'd still be the one alive."

I stare at Dylan's stone while the pastor talks of Jesus. It's a simple stone with an emblem of a tree: GIVER OF LIFE BY DONATION and the engraved BELOVED SON. Rectangular, with saw-toothed edges, it reminds me of a postmark. Perhaps we need a stamp of permanence, to be reminded: "Yes, Dylan was here." He deserves so much more. Maybe I'm glad I'm here. In fact, the last time I was at a family picnic, I didn't want to be there either. It was the last time I heard him say, "I love you, Auntie Kristi." And isn't that how life is sometimes? You either want to be here or you don't. You either have hope, or you don't.

The pastor stops reading and looks over to my sister. "Are you ready to sing your hymn?" And so she sings, not a hymn, but a song by the Dixie Chicks, a song she sang to her son every night, as long as he would let her . . . .

And now the crying really starts. My kids and I are huddled with our arms wrapped around each other's shoulders. My oldest son stands with his feet apart—planted. We lean on him. Just when I think it's over, my other sister, Stacie, comes marching up to the front of the crowd. She's got that determined look on her face and she starts singing "Amazing Grace." Her voice breaks and she sobs. The crowd finishes singing.

And then she starts up again, each word becoming stronger and louder, until she opens up loud and beautiful from somewhere deep and clear, as if she's singing for all of the dead. When she's done, we all clap. "That seems like a fitting enough ending," the pastor says.

People start to disperse, but Shelley stays. I lean into a Pine and watch her. She's lost weight recently. Grief keeps her nauseous. Her eyes are on the cemetery keeper who wears a Vikings jersey and is pushing a rusty wheelbarrow carrying a spade shovel. He digs a hole deep enough for a small tree. He takes a pale yellow rose from a wreath and places the stem into the hole. She stands with her arms crossed, as if she were watching Dylan get his baby shots —something painful that must be done. He places the urn in the grave and gently pats down the black dirt around the petals of the single rose. She nods her head, as if this were her final act, as mother, as gatekeeper. None of us know yet—that she's pregnant. None of us know—that perched inside her uterine cave, rests a drifting embryo. Mysterious and enroute.

My Mother's Hands

1

When I would sit down beside my mother
on a hard piano bench in our entryway room,
her finger-gathering-up hands would cover
and uncover the white and black ivory keys
into melodies, as we sang, "I've got spurs
that jingle jangle . . ." and "Sleigh bells ring,
are you listening . . ." Oh, how I've wished
she would've thought to teach me to play—
not set me down beside another who couldn't.

2

On my surprise rest home visits, when I'd slide
into an empty place beside her at table, I'd cover
her blue-fleshed melody hand with my bird's-nest
hand—all I had retained from my failed lessons—
and she'd say, "Oh," without turning legally blind
eyes from an empty chair across the dining room
table and call me by my childhood family name—
my nickname, as only old relatives at funerals will.
I wish she'd have thought to teach me how to play.

Whether it were at lunch, mid-afternoon game time
or dinnertime, I'd hover momentarily my nested hand
above hers, but with fingers poised, as about to touch
the ivories, before nesting them, *pianissimo*-like, on hers.
But she always knew, as she had learned to play piano
by observing an older sister who had been given lessons.
And when I bent down before leaving for one last kiss,
she'd lift her arms, momentarily place both hands to
either side of my face and, like petals will touch the rim
of a cut glass vase, touch and kiss my down-turned face.

Knots

Rachel came by every morning around ten to have coffee with the old man, check his mood, decide if he'd need a lot or a little attention that day. Sam's been reading Zane Grey lately, having worked through his bookshelf over the winter. Being homebound can be a bitch. Rachel knew how to get Sam to come around to her way of thinking though, and began with easy requests. "Help me pick the border color for this quilt top," she said first. She worked on him little by little over the winter. "Tell me what you think of these colors for a veteran's quilt." By January, Rachel had that old man cutting fabric and piecing squares for a veteran's quilt of his own making to contribute to the cause. At eighty-six, Sam couldn't walk far or breathe well, but he damn sure could still work with his hands. I think back on all the times Sam and I went fishing years ago. He snipped fishing line and tied lures and sinkers to line like nobody's business. How he was able to tie those knots so well, the knots that held walleyes and fighting trout, always amazed me. Sam is tying knots again, not in fishing line, but in thread to make quilts, bent over a sewing machine instead of a fishing boat, his talents too great to silence.

The Orange Tabby Cat

Lord of his domain
master of all he surveys
bringer of trophy heads and
half-dead field mice
scourge of bird-feeders
and neighborhood dogs
the great orange tabby
weary from the day's rounds
sits motionless
eyes half-closed
tail curled around him
basking in the restorative warmth
of the late-afternoon sun

seeing me down the street
he ambles lazily to the curb
leans against my leg when I arrive
responds to my questions
as we approach the door
requires food upon entering
then invites himself up on my lap
for some close personal attention

asked what his rivals would think
if they could see him now
he stretches extravagantly
rolls over to have his belly rubbed
and purrs loudly

Fred did feed the three red deer

Fred did feed the three red deer. That's all we were told. Just type it as you see it. But I didn't know Fred. I didn't know if he even existed. Maybe he didn't like deer. Maybe he even shot them and left them hanging upside down in his yard, as if to embarrass them. Or maybe he loved deer. Lived in the woods with squirrels sitting on his shoulders and sang "Zip-a-Dee-Doo-Dah" all day long, feeding the deer some ferns and salt or whatever it is that deer like for treats. Yeah, that's it. He had a white beard and was sort of chubby with an apple-cheeked face and a merry twinkle in his eyes, full of mirth. Lots of mirth. Ho-ho-ho-ing all day long, tossing ferns and salt about, chatting with the forest animals, knocking the squirrels off his shoulder by accident and then stooping down with his hands on his knees and giving a big belly laugh and even the squirrels were chuckling and amazed by him. Good old Fred. What a guy. How did he ever get into my typing class in junior high school?

It was Mrs. Olafson who introduced us. She was the matronly typing teacher at William Jennings Bryan Junior High School. Home of the Bryan Beavers. That was good for a few smirks. Mrs. Olafson said this would be a good typing exercise. She didn't go into Fred's background. Just told us to do it and smiled in her don't-spill-your-milk-on-my-nice-clean-table kind of smile. So we did it. At least all thirty-eight girls did it. Me, being the only boy in the class, couldn't do it. It wasn't that I wasn't coordinated or anything. Heck, I had taken third place in the ping pong tournament, but typing was a hereditary thing. I had a Y chromosome slipped into me and, as a male, I was destined to be a lousy typist. All males are lousy typists. That is why you don't see war movies about army typists. There were plenty of male army typists. But they were lousy at what they did; otherwise you would have seen John Wayne in *The Keys of Iwo Jima* on late night TV. Fighting and spitting and getting into space-barroom brawls. Or maybe, Gregory Peck in *Shift Lock Hill.*

25

But this is real life, so all you get is me, click clicking away while Virginia Tillsom sits behind me and goes click-etyclickclicketyclickclicketyclick like some Japanese machine gunner in one of those hidden pillboxes on Iwo. But instead of a fifty caliber Kawasaki or whatever, she's got a thiry pound Royal manual. It's really irritating. I'm trying to do Fred some justice here, telling people about his wonderful life feeding the deer, while Virginia Tillsom is rattling off his one line story in endless repetition, sounding like some train clacking on the tracks headed for Nowheresville at breakneck speed and not stopping for any washed-up winos sleeping on the tracks.

She wasn't real pretty, Virginia Tillsom, but she had good features and I might have even asked her to the ninth grade dance, except I never would actually ask her, just *think* about asking her. At this stage of my adolescence, I never asked girls to go to anything. But I would think about which ones I might ask, if I ever got the nerve or a spaceship landed in the schoolyard—whichever happened first. I wondered if she was named after a place in Virginia. Or maybe it was some secret code of her parents, because Mrs. Tillsom got knocked up the first time they did it, as in a virgin till some fateful night. Get it? Hoo boy. But in typing class, she bugged the crap out of me—her with her incessant clickityclickclicking. In algebra class, I got to sit behind her, but what could I do to get even? There was no noisy way to solve a binomial equation.

Unless I could get to the blackboard and screech the chalk down the blackboard at just the right angle—sending the girls and women teachers into moans of hysteria. The screeching didn't seem to bother the boys and men as much as the girls and women. Once I did it with the five piece chalk holder, the one used to make five parallel lines for math and music classes—I held it just right so that all five pieces were screeching at once—I had women teachers racing down the hall to our classroom to get the screeching stopped. All because Mr. Sandbottom, the math teacher, was always out of the room drinking coffee with all the other math/science teachers. So naturally the students thought of all kinds of pranks.

Like Billy Blackstone using the teacher's interoffice phone. The interoffice phone in the classroom was an early model manufactured about two years after A. G. Bell invented the telephone. It had a cloth cord connected to the round receiver and the speaker was built into the wall. Billy used the interoffice phone to perfectly imitate Mr. Sandbottom's voice to call the administrative office and excuse himself for the day for sick leave but was suspended when it was discovered he never saw the school nurse—which he probably avoided because she always made the boys drop their pants so she could check for hernias, even when all you had was a headache or sore throat.

The only time I ever dared go to the nurse was for the annual physical required for boys playing on the athletic teams. They would import a real doctor for a day, who would do about three hundred physicals that day. The only part I can remember is him checking for hernias as he grabbed my nuts while I coughed. This is when the school nurse would "accidentally" walk into the room to supposedly consult with the doctor. Funny how that would happen about one hundred times each day of the physicals. I suppose I should feel honored I made the top 33% to get "interrupted."

What if Virginia Tillsom became a nurse, I daydreamed, and I was a secret agent, reporting in for my annual physical and, you know, she checked me for a hernia and then we fell in love and went off to the woods for our honeymoon. And just as we are about to do it, we get interrupted by this clickityclickclicking noise, and it turns out to be Mrs. Olafson, the typing teacher, clicking her castanets doing the flamenco in the forest with a rose in her teeth and Fred is ho-ho-ho-ing all 'round her wearing tight toreador pants under his bulging belly, with a wide-brimmed Spanish hat with those cloth dingleberries hanging from it, while the deer and the squirrels are jumping all around them, and we are all happy and then . . . I waken from reverie and look up and Mrs. Olafson is staring at the paper in my typewriter carriage, which says nothing but *fjfjfj fjf fjfj fjf jfjfj fjf jfjfj,* over and over and over again. Well, it may not read very well, but I typed it just as fast as Virginia Tillsom.

County 40

Two old men in the clinic waiting room
Meeting once more, maybe one last time for the first time
    again.
One wears a blue cap with some logo in gold,
The other borne to his plastic chair
By an aluminum walker with tennis ball shoes.
I, another old man: a fountain pen,
Blue cap with logo on the chair beside me.
I will not watch, having not been invited,
Not been invited either though, not to listen:

"Old lady who lived back in there off County 40. Name was
    Leona."
"Used to be a resort back there. No more. No more."
"We're putting our place up for sale. Moving into town.
Too far from help if you hurt yourself.
Too far if you don't, come to think."
"Broke my leg." "The wife broke her wrist."
"Yeah, well. But if you break your arm, you can still walk.
Break your leg, you're done."

Now we're all quiet together, done. We're brothers now,
Maybe thinking about those bones. *Them bones* chuckle:
The old health, *them dry bones,* thin dry bones now,
They choose magazines, read at magazines—*Health.*
In honor of our silence, my age and theirs,
I'm done now too, with writing, not brotherhood.
In brotherhood I rise, *hip bone connected* to the creak of
    rejuvenation,
Head back up County 40, the winter drive friable
Like old drought-soil gone mortally sere—
Slick, hard, treacherous bone-white abyss just under the
    glare,
Back to our family's old house, not for sale.
So many things not for sale never seem to be only things.

Roses

The tiger lilies wouldn't stop blooming
for years after she
died. Grandpa doused them with gas and smothered

them with plastic tarps
but still they uncurled their orange spider arms,
to choke the flower beds,

throttle all other flowers. My mother
tried to transplant them
at our house, but they'd never take. To her,

the lilies were Grandma,
her mother, the woman who raised eight
children and never

learned to drive, who dreamed of formal dresses,
Jackie Kennedy,
and that she would walk streets of big cities.

I remember small
things about her, like how she laughed a lot
and smelled like flowers.

Once she left me alone in the bathroom
where the floorboards creaked
beneath my sandals. Above the toilet,

Grandma's powder-can was
at my eye level, so I took the puff
and turned myself white

with powder that smelled like roses. My shoes,
I powdered them, too
so that for days, maybe forever more,

I smelled Grandma in
my soles.

29

The Open Spaces

Sometimes it's when nothing happens
That everything changes. It may be
That in the spaces between the lines
In our little drama we find, or lose,
The eternal diamond.

We walk, talk, speak, act as we
Must, as the world asks and rewards,
And then at the same time it appears.
The audience steps outside, we sink
Into a place without applause.

Then for a moment or a year,
There is silence and stillness;
Life rushes on, but we see it
As if from a distance, question
Our quest.

This is a dangerous time,
And we will never be the same.
In between curtains, the script
Is rewriting itself.

The Wilderness does not care

Torrents of rain boil the surface of the lake
Brawny currents brush back the trees with big storm
    hands
Violent electric veins slice through the green black sky
Air smashing thunder shakes the world, stomps away with
    big storm feet '
Rain steadily drips off the bill of my cap into the soup I am
    stirring
Heavy, muddy rain-soaked clothes thud into piles
Buried treasure of dry gear hastily dug from packs
Young shivering lips huddle close
Constant "is it ready yets" as the comforting smell of hot
    chicken soup gathers
All hungry for a bowl of reassurance

Wrapped in dry clothes, filled with warm soup
Hugged in sleeping bag cocoons
The children are safe, sleeping
Endless gales shake the strong-set tents

Despair works to gather a hold
Against the bond that steadily and silently builds
Wilderness comrades baptized in mud, under the flapping
    tarp
Slogging feet in puddles, holding our coffee cups close
Laughing out loud at the absurdity of it all
Holding our smiles too long
Feeble attempts to cover the worry
Wondering all the "what ifs" as the world around us fully
    rages

Each eventually falls to their own fitful sleep,
Relentless machine gun rain pelts the tents
Night and storm fade to dream . . . .

A collective hallelujah salutes the morning's full power sun
Steam rises on the lake and the ground
We squint, hand-shaded brows, sturdy smiles
Strong hot coffee graciously delivered by a thankful child
Bellies full of breakfast
Clothes hang to dry, worries melt in the balmy air
We made it through this tempest . . . together

Poetry - Scott Stewart

innocence

licks of grass kiss
the bottom of bare feet
assuring the children
they are free

Steaming

The red tip on his cigarette glowed as he smoked and thought.

He stood looking at the street in the steaming Oklahoma night. A wild storm had passed through, leaving the air full of moisture. The huge old trees had tossed and creaked in the wind and the rain had obliterated all other sound for a time. The cool rain on the hot ground had practically sizzled and now created a steamy mist that rose up around the neighborhood. He could barely see the next streetlight. The moist air formed halos around any bit of light. The center of the street gleamed damply with caught light.

He sighed heavily between draws on the cigarette. He knew he should go back inside, finish the argument. Discussion, as she called it. All he knew was that he had needed some air. He came out with her voice ringing in his ears, with his chest tight and his face set in anger. All he could focus on was their rage and the size of what they were talking about, how it mattered so much to them and their future. Things he'd said and should have said rattled inside his head.

Out here, as he breathed in the cool smoothness of the air and then alternately breathed in the dry bitterness of the cigarette smoke, he felt drawn away from their conflict. He felt the heat of the cigarette in his fingers, the roughness of the smoke in his throat and the damp air against his skin. Their words faded away as he felt the air cool around him.

The night had a fairy-tale look. It was unusual for the street to look like this and for him to feel like this. It was as if he had slipped to another country. For an instant, he could sense his smallness on the earth and could sense perhaps his relationship to the world. He was aware of the amazing event of a storm that could transform the street like this, how incredible it was to be alive now in this place, to see this.

He hoped that she had calmed down by now. He wished he could carry this feeling inside to her, wrap it around her, let her know that absolutely nothing was worth hurting each other over.

The red tip on his cigarette glowed as he smoked and thought.

Snow Birds

Outside we have what
Appears to be two colors of snow
On our dormant lawn—
The white, sparkly stuff in the morning sun
And sinister gray in the shadows of
Blue spruces that aren't really blue.
Why should they be? They have the sun and
Their fingers in the rich, chocolate earth—

Our section of paradise is surrounded by
Sections of sway-backed white picket fence
Protruding from the snow-plowed ridge
Along the street with only the
Tips of the pickets showing like
Bleached dinosaur bones guarding our yard
From what? The cold north wind?
Marauding icicle thieves—

Behind the dinosaur bones a pair of naked
Birch stand solitary sentinels, their peeling
Sunburned skin fluttering in the gusty
Breeze like shirtsleeve tatters.
Ravaged by what? Unfulfilled expectations?
Shattered dreams—

Next to our house steam from the
Dryer vent pushes southward on the fingers
Of the jet stream like ghostly spirits
Anxiously seeking warmer climes.
Why not? Is there someplace
We should rather be—

Iceout

Worn tectonic plates four inches thick
Melting into cold slush
Grays under a bulbous pewter sky
I dream awake to such metallic violence

Erupted out of that chilly metaphor of continental
Thrust and succumbing wet movement
Sliding back and forth atop
The inviting depth of heat

But only because I said what I said
To myself and my pen and the smooth ice
Of white paper
For

It is only a lake surface
White ice shifting with wind plowing
A cracked surface to slide over
A gentle gray force of old and tender ice

All no more violent than seasonal melt
No less tender than Earth's roiled surface
In Earth's ancient seasons of ice
Thaw and renewal

And renewal

Summer Flies

Blackflies sneak-attack my sweaty neck,
then disappear before I feel the sting.

I shoo houseflies with a backhand sweep.
They loop and land on my food again.

A horsefly stabs my sunburned arm.
It avoids my slap and I spank raw skin.

Deerflies swarm about my face and ears.
I whip them away with a willow switch.

Dragonflies touch lightly, then dart off—
wanting nothing.

Sacajawea

They call me Bird Woman
a bird without wings
in bondage   as are all women
stolen from my people
slave to the Mandan
wife of Charbonneau
bound to this little man
strapped to my back
only my mind flies free

Great excitement in the village
when pale-skinned men arrive
a big dog and two chieftains
They wait out winter in our earth lodges
tell stories of the Great White Father
in far-off Washington   He sent them
to explore the land of my fathers

I listen as I serve buffalo stew
my heart swells within me
like springtime willow buds
They learn I traveled
these mountains many moons ago
they bargain with Charbonneau
he trades me for coins and firewater

When the river swallows the ice
we begin the upstream journey
With Pompey at my breast
I turn toward the setting sun
and high meadows of my people

The sinews of our trails
lace together the moccasin
of this walking-forward country

Dia de los Muertos

Our house is
too small for this—
the kitchen filled
with friends. Everyone
serves himself
then crowds around
the table. Placemats
overlap, mismatched
silverware clanks,
elbows bump, voices
collide in cross-conversation,
giggles erupt from
the kids' table.

Each November,
we share the food
of our sacred
dead—*tacos al pastor*
and warm corn *tortillas,*
kumlas, halupsi, rice pudding—
telling the stories
of the people
for whom we light
a candle, bring a photo,
say a prayer. This breaking
of bread resurrects the faces
that ours mirror.
Warmth fills this
space, our laughter rises
and lengthens—
this is a celebration.

There is room here
at this old table
for all of our friends.
I hold this moment,
taste it on my tongue
and give thanks.

Allegro Vineyards,
Brogue, Pennsylvania, 1985
In memory of John and Tim Crouch

Emerging from a dip in the rolling Southwestern Pennsylvania landscape, we arrive at a flat dry plain of sorts. Dust spirals behind the car. We keep our windows rolled up and look at each other quizzically, lifting eyebrows. The rows of grape vines look stunted, as if some wood carver had pruned and shaped them into the knuckles of an old man. We wonder at the fine review we'd read earlier in the week about the vineyard's wines.

We follow the dirt road around a squared-off left turn and pass three olive-drab army surplus trailers linked at the nose, looking like a faded cloverleaf. Our hopes sink even lower. At last, we see a small concrete bunker-like building and a small discreet Tasting Room sign. We pull up, the only car, step out, and stretch. A few steps and we are inside an L-shaped room, a short counter straight ahead, an old rag rug of a dog between. From out of the back room steps the man, round-faced and full but stopping short of corpulent, that we will soon be calling John.

He looks nothing like the symphony-musician-turned-vintner we expected. He looks very much the everyday Joe, verging on jolly. We tell him what we imagine will be the magic words, the open sesame. We utter the words "Ray sent us" as if seeking entry to an old-time speakeasy.

Apparently, our friend Ray is an excellent customer, because John introduces himself and explains that he and his brother live in those trailers. One tends the vines, the other the wines. John begins the sampling, matching us wine for wine. For every varietal and bottling—Vidal, Seyval—he has the perfect recipe in mind. He is clearly a connoisseur of food and wine and music, if not high fashion.

We fall into his easy-going spell; the dog thumps his tail and sighs. Being purists (aka wine snobs), we are surprised that our favorite wine is a peach blend called Celeste. I can summon it still today and feel that summer on my tongue, breathe its delicate scent. From such a sullen place, drab utilitarian trailers, dry fields, cement block, such symphony. It is optimism at its best to imagine such pleasantness, honey, peach, cork, green bottle, wind chimes, fresh pie could come from this.

We visited Allegro Vineyards often that summer, and the next and then moved out of state. A few years ago, I read that John and Tim Crouch had both passed away and the winery sold. I can't imagine Pennsylvania without them, without Allegro Seyval Blanc, without peach-scented Celeste. Pennsylvania without the Crouch brothers just doesn't seem right. It would be like Minnesota without lakes, without loons.

Poetry - Niomi Rohn Phillips

Morning Glory: Faith Renewed

The fragile tendrils
strive for life
in early spring.
In midsummer
aggressive vines
escape the lattice
cling to cosmos
bend it to the ground
with lush foliage and
promise of flowers.
Then
in the stillness
of September dawn
the trumpets open.

Poetry - Rhoda Jackson

Ode to Miss Emily D.

I met you on the road to Immortality,
pausing in Hope's Garden,
where your metaphors blossomed
and nestled in my Heart.

There among the Brambles,
a kindred Soul offered a basket of Friendship;
Preceptor selecting her new Scholar

Possibility is my companion now,
finding circumference of Meaning
glowing brighter than any gemstone;
Lighting the Path towards Truth.

Cats of the Eastern Mediterranean

In Civitavecchia, a suburb of Rome,
at the bed and breakfast, after breakfast,
a first cat sighting: a gray pouf of smoke,
slitted yellow eyes, stretched out blandly
under the awning in the flag-stoned shade.
No cats were noticed in Croatia,
but lots of old brick and Catholic crosses.
The Corfu cats were as elusive
as the legend of Odysseus's boat,
a rock off the coast of Paleokastritsa.
In Katakolon, beach cats roamed the sand,
chasing wet windblown weeds—
hunting for fish tossed onto the shore.

They wrapped themselves around columns
in Corinth, padded through ancient ruins,
stood where Paul confronted the Corinthians.
Turkish cats were as plentiful as prayers
wrapped in white cloth and tied
to a fence next to the house of Jesus's mother.
I spied a clever cat at ancient Ephesus,
one with markings: a dark crown on its head,
striped tail wrapped around antique white body,
owning a place among the tourists near the library.
And then the silly tabby Kusadasi cat near port,
lying under a store window, shopped out
from all the haggling, sidewalk-sleeping
on its back, wrapped in cool and quiet shadow.

At the highest point on volcanic Santorini,
a black and white cat lounged under ripe figs,
unmoved by the noisy tourists' oohs and ahhs
while landscape stretched out into the ocean
like an advertisement for a dream come true.
I did not see the cavorting Coliseum cats of Rome,
no Catacomb cats, or even holy cats posed
at Papal sightings. But they were nosing around,
no doubt, sniffing as we were, the odors of antiquity.
Cats so conspicuously absent from the bible,
live outdoors, year-round among the relics,
roll nonchalantly in ancient history's dust and toil.

Red's Garden

Red did his job down at the plant for three and a half decades, managing various materials and turning them into useful products. He then spent the next sixteen years in his garden, managing the weeds and turning out the hardiest vegetables in the neighborhood. Now the cancer was doing its job, managing his thoughts and turning his insides into useless dead cells.

He disliked the new town doctor. He was young, half Red's age, addressing Red always as "Mr. Merman," with a heavy Eastern European accent, giving the front end of Red's last name a "mirror" pronunciation rather than the proper "myrrh."

"The tests came back positive," the doctor told him in a tone as sterile as the office, and on a pristine winter morning that would have otherwise found Red lounging, drinking coffee with his wife Gale, followed by a visit to the senior center for a few rounds of cribbage with long-time friends. Something clicked hard in Red's mind at the sound of the words. It dawned on him that the doctor had been calling him a "mere man" for however many visits.

As Red walked back outside, into the cold, he pondered his finitude, his mortality, as a "mere man." How does a mere man go out with a bang? In the giant scheme of things, seventy years is a long time, he figured, but still, a man just doesn't call it a day and wave the grim reaper over for one last beer.

Over recent years, he'd heard and watched many others who had toiled alongside him at the plant, cut down by the same hatchet. He wondered if it made sense to think about what could have been. The paper mill had job openings as well, but the manufacturing plant was paying more per hour. He felt a twinge of bitterness as he thought about how those guys at the paper mill had it easy, nothing but slivers to hazard. Worst case: lose an arm in one of the machines. They had never had to worry about something as ghastly as the ill effects of asbestos.

As Red drove home, he thought about a chance conversation with a young woman with dark hair and brown eyes, standing with friends beneath the marquee of the Chief Theatre. He could still remember bits and pieces, made up of awkward phrases and buttery-popcorn sarcasm, dreams of the Big Leagues and Marlon Brando, as he stood there, a gangly youth a year out of high school, stiff in his oft-worn town team baseball jersey, self-promoting.

Red would kiss the girl later that summer, on the steps of the old locomotive in Fauley Park, just as the stars sprouted through the dark skies over the quiet Midwestern town. And then she would bless him with three daughters.

"They'll bury me before I can bury those seeds," he mumbled to himself, now staring at the foot-high snow blanketing his garden like an unwelcome tarp.

A form of remission kept the beast's destructive nature at bay and into spring. Signs of hope filled Red's mornings, while the sounds of visiting grandchildren and great-grandchildren filled the air.

Red walked ahead of Gale to the garden, dropping at the corner where the first row of tomatoes would begin.

"Red, you're going to get your pants dirty." There was a cheery tone in her scolding.

He could feel the cold dampness of the earth seeping through his khakis and into his knees. He didn't care. It was May and he was alive. Later that month, he stood in his living room for a moment of silence for the passing of his favorite baseball player, Harmon Killebrew.

Red's health saw peaks and valleys through the course of the early summer. Like his health, he watched the Twins on TV struggling through the course of their season, moving up a position one week and down two the next. Red knew he too was moving one step forward, only to fall two steps back. But the important thing was his vegetables were progressing, on course, in spite of the late start. The cornstalks were knee high by the fourth of July. Invigorated by the sight, he and Gale brought lawn chairs to sit near the curb and watch the parade along Main Street. It was one last opportunity to pay homage to a town, a community which had, overall, provided him with a grand life.

August came, warm and dry, putting Red on notice. Both his strength and appetite were waning, as his trembling hand moved the spraying nozzle of the garden hose across his thirsty garden.

"You're tired, Grandpa. Let me do that."

To Red's ears, the voice of his eldest grandchild, Rachel, was filled with youth and the promise of the future. The warm breeze carried the scent of her perfume, sending Red back in time, to a place where old age and dying were so distant, a place that reminded Red of his time to grow, to prosper, to be in love, and to give thanks to God for it all.

He handed her the nozzle and stepped aside.

There would be a harvesting, but Red knew he would not have the energy to fill baskets of corn and squash and cucumbers. The beast inside was winning the war. He could feel his every desire ebbing away.

He stepped up onto the porch, seeing Gale smiling.

"She means well," Gale told Red.

He placed his hand on her soft cheek, her eyes betraying her emotions, as she stumbled through the sentence, "God knows it'll always be your garden, Red." He caught her tear in his palm and smiled, proud of having had a hand in those things growing both above and beneath the ground.

"There's a garden in a quiet neighborhood." The minister spoke above the whispering breeze and beneath the shade of the tallest elm in the Merman's backyard. "You can find it just this side of town, where the sidewalks end and near the woods, stirring with deer and squirrel, where birds perch among the lindens and poplars. The garden's bright colors stir the appetite. The swelling of zucchini, squash, corn, tomatoes and cucumbers liven the neighborhood. Family and friends, on a day of remembrance and thanks, will taste—once baked or boiled or roasted—the bounty provided by the absent gardener.

"The man was his garden," the minister continued. "It's said that a man makes of himself from what he takes from the earth. This man planted, cultivated, and wrested

from the land bushels and bushels of the heartiest vegetables. Red wanted to be here but couldn't. The Almighty
holds sway over the last of the seeds, the ones well known
for their endless bounty, like a waterfall, plunging long and
forever. Amen.

"Let us eat."

Poetry - Bob Sullivan

After Your Death

the sirens break
the silence
of the night.

the raindrops
on my window

remind me
that you
are still here.

Poetry - Marlene Mattila Stoehr
Honorable Mention

After the Funeral

Family and neighbors lingered
around the old oak table.
They drank cups of strong coffee,
ate bologna sandwiches,
nibbled at large squares of frosted cake,
talked about the weather,
and fell into prolonged silences.
They were delaying the time they must leave.
Everyone knew and no one wanted to say it.
Things had changed forever in that house.

Emma circled the table,
refilling coffee cups that were only half-empty,
then walked wearily to the window
and stood beside the wooden kitchen chair,
his chair.

Still dressed in funeral clothes,
without her usual apron
with a pocket harboring a handkerchief,
she reached for the hem of the ruffled white curtain,
gently wiping her eyes
and returned to serving her guests.

January Snow

The snow floats
like feather confetti,
two feet of down
rounding all edges
to softness.

Not like snow
my father remembered
when Dakota wind
ruthlessly blew blizzard across
Minnesota for days,
blinding everything white.
Cattle were lost,
tracks covered in seconds.
Grandfather strung a rope
from house to barn
so boys doing chores
could find their way back.
People died in that snow.

This snow stills breath
with grace,
thrills mind with wonder.
Pristine beauty,
welcome as praise.

The Gap Between Us

In Minneapolis,
A dog in our care runs ahead of us,
Snow mists a steeple
In the dusk.
There is much I can't tell you.

I look at the church doors
Large dark brown wood,
They do not open.
It is then I feel the gap
Between us.

You belong in the mountains,
Splinters of wood to hold up your life.
Perhaps the Rockies looking for
Peace in the whitening sky,
Among the hard rocks.

Here I belong
Watching the snow mix with dirt
The exhaust of a timid life.

You tell me
The city extinguishes us.
No one watches for forest fires
From those distant brick buildings
The dog would love to disappear among.
You say a city is a kind of wilderness
Especially here, lone wolves
Waiting, stalking at the bus stops.

I hope for a closeness
That will not exist.
A prevailing theme in my life.
The distance as unyielding
As that brick church, whose
Brownish-red (as if baked) walls
Stare down at us, denying entry. As if
I was asking for salvation
Without the act of what I did not have:
Prayer.

My Path

Sometimes it was level,
Clearly defined.
At other times
It meandered
Unsure of
Which direction
To take.
Afraid of heights,
Trying desperately
To ascend mountain paths
Meant for sure-footed goats.
Sometimes so dense with brush
It needed to be cleared
As I went,
Making progress slow.
Often like a foggy morning,
My vision impaired by mist,
Groping along,
Trying to find my way
Through a maze,
Running into obstacles
Like one who is blind.
The taste of fear
Strong in my mouth.
Learning to pick myself up
And start over again.
And again.

Ghost Writing

He hung blank sheets of paper on the refrigerator, his office door, the clothesline in the backyard, the silver snout of the bathtub faucet. If you looked closely at the paper, at the right angle, in the proper degree of moderate sunlight, you could see letters, glyphs, words, phrases, whole paragraphs, written with some otherworldly, spectral ink.

The first ones appeared on computer paper he left on the clothesline. Outside, there were whirlwinds of words floating around, captured on the paper from lone ghosts and free-floating ideas. He quickly wrote the words down, documenting the date and time of every discovery. Unlike EVP, he was not limited to recording sounds in cemeteries, old houses, and hovering "cold spots." He became a new kind of recorder, a reader of invisible words, a word whisperer.

He papered up every square inch of his house, even the aquarium and dog kennel. His office walls and windows were wallpapered with stray parchment, all in the hope of capturing words. Finally, he applied yellow sticky notes over every visible portion of his body and closed his eyes. Letter by letter the words manifested themselves on every sticky note, words from one yellow square colliding with words from another. The creep of alphabet crawls over his skin, each manifesting new wounds, new meaning.

Minnesota Avenue—First Snow

The cold drapes ferns of frost
along the porch rail—
decorating for Thanksgiving.

Noisy clowns
in brightly colored costumes,
complete with red noses
and penguin feet,
wait for the big yellow bus
to take them to the circus.

Dog-walkers
tote white grocery bags
filled with steaming "gifts."

We drag out saucers and snowboards
to harvest fun from the cold

And at the end of the day,
we are grateful for home
and tiny marshmallows.

Nailed

My roommate Jodi refuses to go to the doctor. Ever. She also mocks me for frequent doctor visits for minor afflictions. When I had a cold this winter, I went in for antibiotics. Jodi, who is three years my junior at forty, followed with a similar cold but refused to see a doctor. Instead, she coughed her way through it and, after several weeks, recovered.

Jodi grew up a Wisconsin farm girl, whereas I grew up a suburbanite from Bloomington, Minnesota. Did that farm upbringing make Jodi tougher than me?

One Friday, Jodi took off work and drove to the farm to do chores. She was moving boards when a rusty nail sticking out of a board punctured her foot. The nail went in a half inch.

It made her sick to her stomach, but Jodi looked at her watch and got back to work.

Later, her mom noticed something amiss. "Why is your foot wet?"

"It's nothing," Jodi replied, not wanting to worry her mom, but the blood had seeped through her sock.

After driving home an hour and a half to the Cities, Jodi hurried over to a friend's house for happy hour. The motherly hostess soaked Jodi's foot in warm water with Epsom salt, then swaddled it in bandages.

Limping in around 11 p.m., Jodi bragged how her friend had cleaned the wound.

I eyed the foot suspiciously. "Maybe you should have a doctor look at it."

"I'm fine." Jodi waved.

The next morning at 8 a.m., these words eked from the hallway: "I need to go to the doctor."

I shot out of bed.

I stumbled for my pants, grabbed my glasses, threw on a sweatshirt. "Where to?"

"Riverside. I need a Fairview Clinic so they can check my tetanus records." Jodi clenched her teeth while easing on clunky winter boots because her swelled foot wouldn't fit into her loafers. She hobbled to the front door, nearly crawling. "Should we stop for some coffee?"

Coffee? Was she nuts? She could barely walk. She could *lose* her *foot.* And she wanted *coffee?*

I was already wide-awake.

"We don't need to stop."

"No, let's get coffee."

We fueled up at Holiday, then sped off to Riverside. But the place was a zoo of construction zones. We circled for fifteen minutes until we found the Urgent Care.

"Shoot. It's not a Fairview Clinic," I said. "Well, let's try Southdale."

"Okay." She sounded eerily calm, sipping her hazelnut Brazilian roast.

Was she really okay?

"What year is it?"

"2011."

"What day?"

"Saturday."

"Who's the president?"

"Unh." An eye roll followed the grunt.

Whew. She was still lucid.

Fifteen minutes later, at Fairview Southdale, Jodi read the hours on the door: Saturdays 1 p.m. to 8 p.m.

It was only 8:45 a.m.

"We'll try Bloomington. I know right where it is." I had been there for a bug bite that summer. A nice doctor there handled my case and assured me I'd recover. "If they aren't open, Apple Valley has a 24-hour Urgent Care. There's also Highland."

In Bloomington, we only waited a couple minutes.

"Jodi," the nurse called.

On Pavlovian reflex, I stood up and followed the nurse while Jodi trailed behind.

The nurse quickly took Jodi's vitals, then reviewed her records. "Your last tetanus was in 2005."

When the doctor dashed in, I recognized her as the same one who had treated my bug bite. "This could be *very* serious. You should have come in sooner," she scolded.

I tensed, gripping my plastic chair. Jodi was going to lose her foot or *die!*

"*I* told her to come in last night," I said.

Jodi was quieter than she'd ever been.

The doctor unraveled mummy-like bandages and examined the puncture.

"We'll need X-rays."

They hauled Jodi off to radiology.

You can judge the seriousness of an illness by how long they make you wait. Jodi was in the express lane for this one. I'd brought a book but hadn't even gotten through a single page when the door opened. Jodi hop-shuffled back in and plunked down.

Soon, the doctor returned.

"You were lucky. The X-rays look good, but there's still a fragment in your foot. I want to clean it again. Do you want a numbing shot?"

Jodi nodded.

The doctor pulled on plastic gloves and goggles.

"Lie on the table."

The white paper rustled as Jodi slid onto it. Then the doctor pushed a four-inch needle into Jodi's foot. Blood dripped from the entry point.

Jodi shrieked. Tears streamed down her cheeks.

"Hold her leg down."

I leaned all my weight above Jodi's knee.

Jodi cried, "It *hu-ur-urts.*"

"Think of a happy place." I pressed harder, fighting her kick-reflex. "You're on the beach; it's sunny; there's sand. *You'reonthebeeeeeeeeeaaaaach!*"

Jodi spilled more tears. That was the numbing shot?

I dropped into my chair. Was this really the same doctor who had so tenderly handled my bug bite?

A magnifying glass hung from the doctor's forehead like a miner's work light. The doctor scraped the foot and dug out the last molecule of dirt. Then she bandaged the wound while Jodi gasped to catch her breath.

"Keep that foot elevated. It speeds healing." The doctor snapped off her gloves, then prescribed antibiotics. "You can expect some pain and redness, but watch for infection."

I looked at a reddened hangnail on my pinky. "Would it look like this?" Maybe they would want to examine me, too.

"That's normal healing. It would be an angry red."

What would that look like? Maybe someone's thumb a hammer had accidentally nailed.

"Come in right away next time," the doctor said, her demeanor turning sweeter. "Any deep cut in the foot can be serious."

Now Jodi would have to slow down her crazy work schedule, I snickered.

But that fanatical farm girl returned to work the next day. Maybe she *was* tougher than me.

At home, I examined my hangnail. Was the redness getting worse? Suddenly, I envisioned that four-inch needle plunging into my pinky. Nah, I'd be fine after all.

Practice Session

Downhill from the Minneapolis Institute of Arts,
past Fair Oaks Park, almost to Franklin Avenue,
three young men with long white canes sweep
the sidewalk side to side like treasure hunters
with metal detectors a sandy beach for coins,
wedding rings—that sizzle crackle of discovery.
One man wears heavy-framed, dark sunglasses;
the other two, blindfolded, as with sleep masks
wealthy women in films wear, coffered women
no man watching imagines men make love to.
I'm struck by the length of each extended cane,
as by one-legged stands of Lesser Heron Cranes
in shallows of ponds and at reedy edges of lakes.
When we look again, they approach the curb:
their canes hesitate, and then both in blindfolds
step out into Franklin Avenue, as if into water
without knowing whether it is shallow or deep.
They are learning to listen for that crackle sizzle,
to be still and to trust as the Lesser Herons trust.

Waiting

Today, I touched a red dragonfly,
so still I thought it was dead.

It flew off in the direction of tomorrow,
moving faster than my startled eyes could follow.

The garden and lawn are thick
with leaves, choked with the leavings of fall.

The bare trees reach skyward,
the fallen leaves speak crisply in the wind

like old bones,
all of us old bones and the dust of broken leaves—

we are waiting.
This weather is too warm for October,

though I hold tight to the heat,
storing it in my cells.

I can't precisely remember the long winter
but it haunts me.

I can't go anywhere without flowers leaning
at me amid the dead things

and fat bees circling, their angry cousins,
the hornets and wasps close behind. We are all out of sorts

with this strange reprieve, this sullen heat,
that keeps us up nights, waiting

as we do, not for what we need
but for what we have come to expect.

The Feather and the Stone

I live alone and, although I wish I didn't, at least I have things pretty much the way I want them. I come and go, eat and sleep, whenever it suits me. One of my habits involves the small TV table where I eat my at-home meals. Beside the silverware and napkin rest two special items: a feather and a stone. Although they fight with the food for space on the crowded tray, I never dine without them.

A few years back a package arrived in the mail. After taking off the postal packaging, I was delighted to find the most prettily wrapped gift box in memory. The dark maroon crepe paper made a stark visual contrast with the black silk ribbon embracing it. And the rough feel of crepe counterbalanced the satiny smooth tie. But what crowned the ensemble was a bright crimson feather protruding jauntily from the bow. The overall effect was stunning, so much so that I hesitated to spoil the effect by opening the package. But I did and, handsome as they were, paper and ribbon were discarded. But that red feather, it had captured my heart. So it has stayed on to share my company at mealtime, a bright reminder of a pleasant moment in time.

The stone is really nothing special. It's just a small curio I picked up long ago at some seaside gift shop. Mottled gray and about two inches long, it is highly polished, at least on the part that shows. The unseen bottom on which it rests was not deemed worthy of polishing, so the beachcomber simply left it rough. My original thought was that this keepsake would end up on my desk as a paperweight, but it had a different destiny.

Early on, I got the notion that the stone's neglected and unappreciated bottom needed a little tender loving care on my part. That turned into quite a polishing project. No emery paper and rubbing compound would do; this would be just between me and the stone. So I got in the habit of picking it up at odd moments and, holding it upside down in my hand, passing my thumb back and forth over the rough surface. Our stairway banister had gotten shiny smooth from years of similar hand rubbing, so why not my stone? It was just something I'd do while otherwise engaged in reading, watching the tube, whatever.

After years of effort, I must solemnly announce that the stone's underbelly is no smoother than the day I brought it home. There are no signs of progress at all. A thumb, apparently, is no match for a stubborn lump of ten-million-year-old glacial grit. But, oddly enough, the stone has done wonders for the thumb and the person attached to it.

All the time I was sitting there trying to smooth it, that pampered pebble was busy smoothing me. The simple repetitive motion of stroking the grainy surface had a definite calming effect, banishing the cares of the day and leaving me in gentle repose. The more I rubbed, the better I felt. Aladdin's lamp, rubbed in similar fashion, could have done no more. In gratitude, it now occupies a prime spot near the salt shaker.

So there they sit on my tray, nature's odd couple. To most people, contrasting symbols of fragility and durability, but to me they represent beauty and happiness. They keep me company at mealtime, each contributing to my sense of well-being in its own way. They make my defrosted pot pie taste like a sirloin steak.

In case you're still wondering what was in that gift box, so am I. I haven't a clue.

Yes, I still rub.

Inked in Winter

I watch lithe, young Joe
stroll Le-pe-eu-lē Beach
red, green, purple on bronze
a walking Gauguin
body art Retrospective

> full sleeves, both calves
> surfer short tattoos
> a lei necklace
> an anchor at belly, a broken chain
> *leaving New York, coming*
> *out of the closet, aloha*

> a snake entwined in a rose, sugar skull
> with cherry blossoms, a blue bird
> *the danger of beauty, the lure of evil,*
> *the import of happiness*

> lion, dragon, bulldogs
> Satan and saint
> *courage, wisdom, conscience*

I should brave the barbed needle
etch geography, history
and philosophy of long life
on my wrinkled wrap

clothe the story
in Minnesota winter
a secret Retrospective
when memory fades

Checking Out

He can't remember
his grandkids,
misspells his daughter's
married name.
They come
to wash his windows,
trim the hedges, shovel
snow. He no longer
drives. He has packed
his funeral clothes,
set out the photos
for the display
his children will
arrange at the wake.
His dead wife's nightgown
hangs on the back
of the bathroom door
like a fragile forget-me-not
pressed between pages. He has
nowhere to go but home.

Goodbye, Dad

Words unsaid between us, a last chance.
He was dying. Did only one of us know?
Later, at his visitation, a stranger told me
Dad confided he was not going to make it.

Sitting by his bedside there were things
I needed to know, so much I wanted to say.
*Forgive me for the one time I hurt you
on purpose;* the apology caught in my throat.

Dad was the bright star of my childhood.
That day at Mary's wedding, everything
provided for her, I wanted to strike out at him
for loving his step-daughter more than me.

When his long-time friend Turner left
I told Dad the years were kinder to Turner.
It wasn't true. Dad was as handsome
as ever, the mischief glinting in his eyes,

with that touch of vulnerability loved by
women. Instead, I asked why he hadn't
gotten me professional help when I was
the problem child, making it impossible

to keep household help after Mother died.
Genuine surprise lit his eyes. He said,
"Why, you turned out all right." A single
compliment held dear all the years since.

Poetry - Cheryl Weibye Wilke
Pots and Pans

I love the way the outdoor lamp
of my house shines through the darkness
of my rooms at night. In the same
way, I love recalling the clanking
sound of pots and pans
as my mother put them away long after
her children went to bed. I
find comfort in the golden
halo of nighttime and those silver
bells of sound. They both
lull me to sleep and keep
me awake with her memory.

Poetry - Sonja Kosler
Haiku

white swan feathers drift
snow begins silent season
visible breath slows

Long Winter

For a week, the weatherman had been warning of an atmospheric disturbance heading northward, carrying with it the possibility of accumulating snow. But this, who could have guessed?

It started in the evening two days before Halloween as wind-whipped flurries. The local forecast said to expect up to five inches of the white stuff by morning. The flurries turned into a whiteout, piling up at an inch per hour. Two days later the snow quit falling, leaving the north woods buried beneath a blanket that wouldn't disappear until late March, and it was hardly November.

Pete had always been a loner, even more so after his wife Jana had passed away. Ten years ago, he sold everything they had owned and moved to a four-room log cabin in the remote reaches of Minnesota. Other than an infrequent twenty mile trip into town for necessities, he had little contact with the outside world.

Over the years, he and his two children had become progressively more estranged. Neither he nor they had made any attempt at contact for over three years. They took life paths that angled away, never intersecting.

The day the "big dump" ended, Pete dug his way out the back door, shoveled a path to the woodshed, and pushed open the ramshackle door. As he was loading his arms with billets of split firewood, he felt something brush his leg. A scrawny black cat, its tail held high in the air, rubbed against him and purred.

Pete pushed it away with his foot.

"Where the H did you come from? Scoot! Get out of here! The last thing I need is a damn animal to take care of," he railed.

Menacingly, Pete stomped his foot, and the cat fled out the door into the deep snow, where it turned and issued a pathetic meow. Pete ignored its plea and trudged by to fill his wood box. It would be a cold one tonight, the forecaster said.

The next morning Pete made his daily trip to the shed. The cat had found its way back in, and again Pete chased it outside into the snow.

"Get out of here, you mangy thing. I don't need you around."

Every day the sun rose later and set earlier, and every day the temperature dropped lower. It seemed to snow every day and inches of the white stuff turned to feet. Every day, Pete and the cat repeated the same scenario, Pete cursing and chasing the cat and the cat pleading for help.

The woodshed was a perfect place for mice to survive and, after every snowfall, they left their footprints, tiny dots in the snow, as evidence of their presence. Eventually, Pete noticed that the tracks in the snow around the woodshed were becoming fewer and fewer. Eventually there were none. The cat grew thinner.

"Get out of here, you bag of bones," Pete said as he brushed it away. "If I feed you, you'll just stick around. Get it? I don't want you!" But the cat didn't leave.

One day, Pete began to push the cat away, but it stretched up on its hind legs, wrapped its front legs around Pete's in a desperate hug, and wouldn't let go. Pete tried to shake it off, but the cat hung on with the last bit of energy left in its body. He stooped and picked up the wisp of a thing and tucked it under his jacket.

"You damn animal. If I leave you out here, you're going to die. Then I'll have that to think about."

With the cat under his coat and a load of wood in his arms, Pete stomped back to the cabin. He felt the cat purring next to his chest.

He found some scraps left over from breakfast, put them in a bowl, and set them on the floor.

"Hey, don't eat so fast. You'll choke to death or throw up. Either way I don't want the mess," he groused.

When the cat finished wolfing down the scraps, it came over to where Pete was sitting and rubbed against his leg. Pete lifted it onto his lap where the cat curled up in contentment.

"No claws?" Pete said in bewilderment as he fingered the front paws of the cat. He turned the cat to look at its backside. "Looks like somebody took care of that, too. You must have belonged to someone once.

"Well, I suppose you need a name. How's Drifter sound to you, seeing as how you sort of drifted in with the blizzard?"

Pete was accustomed to winter in the northland, shorter days, longer nights, colder temperatures and gray skies, but this year was different. Confining snow had fallen too early.

His cabin was at the end of a Forest Service road that wasn't plowed in winter, and he had no one who would miss him if he didn't show up in town. Pete had enough food stored away and enough firewood to last until spring, but he was stranded and alone, except for Drifter.

Christmas and New Year's passed, as did most of January, and Drifter gained weight until Pete could hardly feel his ribs when he stroked the cat's glossy black fur. Pete didn't fare as well.

The persistent grip of depression started as a general sadness but, as the winter progressed and his confinement continued, Pete thought more and more of questions he had faced before and had stuffed inside. Now, he couldn't stuff them in his psychological closet.

What good is life? Why couldn't I have died when she did? Where are my kids?

By the time February was a memory, Pete was in deep depression, so deep he had no desire to make meals for himself, no desire to get out of bed in the morning. All will for living had left him.

But each morning Drifter would be there, rubbing against Pete's face. Each night he'd curl up on top of the covers next to Pete, and Pete would reach over and feel the cat's vibrating purr. Each day, Pete would force himself to get out of bed to care for the cat. He would compel himself to bring in one more load of wood to heat the cabin for "that damn cat."

Winter gave one more push to break those who live up north. For a week, the red line of the thermometer didn't reach above zero, but one day the wind changed.

Pete held Drifter in his arms, petting him as they watched water drip off the ends of the icicles hanging from the eaves. The sun was warm through the window and he looked down at the cat. They both soaked in the promise of spring.

"What do you say, old friend? Should we call the kids when the road is clear?"

Snowfall

On my way home tonight, I was driving
in a gentle, but steady snowfall just beginning

to lay her blanket across the road. Up to four
inches through the night, a blank face

on the radio rambled matter-
of-factly. There was so much noise

inside the car. I yearned to hear
just the snow. It has been so long. I turned

off the radio. Still so much noise. I turned
off the heat. Yet the tires crunched

and the wipers marched
back and forth to shake and knock

chunks of ice all about. So much noise.
I wondered, if I were to pull over

             and stop
and turn it all off . . .

what would I hear? It has been so long
that I can not remember—

so much noise—yet
I have not forgotten the peace

to be found in the madly intricate
face of snow.

Good Words

Reading exceptionally authored
publications, confronted by
unexploited ambiguous words

Underlined or scribbled into trusty
notebooks, rediscovered weeks later,
thereafter scrutinized and absorbed

I feel rich, learning new judicious
delicious words—hook, line
and sinkering me into reading on . . .

Caterwaul, the tattered page reads
four dogs yelping in the bowels
of the basement, a *dybbuk* spirit

Testing the soul, the *physiognomy*
of the landscape seen through
a *pince-nez* in a *homburg* world.

My overcrowded head continues
digesting esoteric words stretching
my brain into a *rhomboid*, the *moribund*

Nature of the blue ribbon words,
causing me to query their lasting effect . . .
"Time will tell," the *pugilist* shares,

His *coruscating* eyes promising
good words make one feel . . .
jaw-dropping, filthy rich.

Dared to Swim

I remember being under water
looking up
and seeing the underside of ripples
shimmering,
as I realized—again—I couldn't swim.
So I kept holding my breath
and walked the lake bottom toward shore,
my cousins and siblings screaming laughter
when my head first appeared,
as if floating on the water's surface.

I looked back at our lake,
while pulling myself up on the dock,
and my eight-year-old heart knew
there would be consequences;
the watchers in that boat I'd jumped off
would not let me forget I had failed again.

I never told them
it wasn't their words that hurt the most—
it was losing sight of sunlight
dancing through underwater ripples.

Memories of Duluth

A couple years ago
on a hotel patio
facing Lake Superior,
I jotted the notes.
Cleaning some drawers
today, I found the list:
Purple petunias . . .
they surrounded the doorway.

A horse-drawn cart,
teens running backward,
a group sauntering, singing,
woman drinking coffee,
storing hot-cup in her purse . . .
all this on the boardwalk
at shoreline with red,
black, white mottled stones.

To the east, a lighthouse,
west, the famous drawbridge.
On the flat horizon, a freighter.
Close in, water sparkling
as evening settled.
Gulls scratching, soaring.

Up-shore, motels,
some with balconies.
Off-shore, an askew building
I'm told is an old, preserved,
fish-cleaning house.

Before me, convention ladies,
many seniors, are making S'mores
at an open grill, hotel provided.

My list ends with "errant dandelion,"
memory falters . . .
perhaps in the grass,
perhaps in the petunias.

Time Goes On

A sleek marble stone with your name is all I have left
A reminder embedded atop all my hopes and dreams.
To have had you once in my life just wasn't enough
I still long to have you with me each and every day

Time seems to just drag on; I don't remember it being this
        way
It's as if when you left, a weight was attached to hold time
        back
The sky stays a deep gray, just as it was a year ago today
It's almost like night in the middle of the day

The air thick with the smell of trying-to-rain
Knowing that I sit here, luckily it waits.
Leaving this spot is always the hardest to do
I'm being forced to say goodbye all over again

My heart being shattered into splinter-size pieces
As if it was a mirror carelessly dropped on the floor.
They say with time it won't be this way
But who are they to say anything at all
They just don't know that time has stalled
Stuck and holding up traffic at a green light.

And a Bier For Dad

So here I am, walking up the church aisle again, half-wishing I would have stayed home. This time I'm behind her, the widow, instead of in front of her, the bride. I was flower girl when she married Dad thirty-five years ago, happy to be a part of the wedding, to wear my new organdy dress with eyelet ribbons and tiny buttons. Happy until I saw her daughters, junior bridesmaids, in long satin gowns.

That day years ago, my stepmother wore a white gown; today, she wears gray wool. Her walk is the same—unsteady then in white heels, unsteady now in black Hush Puppies. She leans into the daughter beside her, the surviving daughter. The other, dead from an overdose years ago, was sent to The Great Beyond with a quiet funeral mass attended by family and a few tattooed fellow travelers.

Today, the front pews are occupied, the center of the church empty, the rear a haphazard array of singles. Although it's September, the church feels like a giant walk-in cooler, a vacant damp cold. I recognize Dad's fishing buddies in their black rayon Al's Bait Shop jackets, his fellow union members from Federal Cartridge, the Knights of Columbus honor guard in creased white shirts and navy polyester pants. What are they doing here? Dad wasn't a KC. I smell coffee brewing in the basement, and suddenly crave a stimulating jolt of caffeine.

Look at the morning sun glint through the stained glass windows. Look at the brilliant patches of greens and reds and blues on the white shirts of the KCs and on the white banners—HUSBAND AND FATHER—draped on the coffin. Look at the bouquets and wreaths that dot the altar. Why these? This group of mourners doesn't look prosperous enough to afford them. Why the expensive casket? Why the funeral mass, for God's sake? I think I know who funded this party. We all have an image to protect.

The organist struggles with "Nearer My God to Thee." I was thinking "Another One Bites the Dust." At my stepsister's funeral where the ushers passed the collection plate, Dad said it would be a cold day in Hell before he went back to this church. Maybe I should call him and ask about the temperature down there.

Father Conroy reminded Mother that he would ask for reminiscences of the departed during the funeral mass. I pray that she will resist the temptation. She's honed a litany of husbandly and fatherly attributes over the last few days and at the wake last night. Before they were married, did he really offer his house to her when she was evicted from her apartment? Did he really give her the keys to his pickup when her car was repossessed? And the rose story —a fresh rose every day in the truck, on the front door knob of the house, on her desk at the Credit Union. Was that true? Who cares? Remind me to never trust a man who sends a rose every day.

Dad. We achieved our final degree of separation the day he lit up a Marlboro in my baby's bedroom. I grabbed the cigarette, bumped the beer bottle out of his hand, and gave him the choice of reprogramming his bad habits or staying away. He didn't return.

So here we are, the "survived by . . ." crowd. We take our seats in the front pew. Father Conroy walks down from the altar, forces a lame smile, and reaches for Mother's hand. I'm embarrassed and touch the hem of my leather skirt, tugging it to my knees. Father wears a white damask stole with intricately embroidered red-orange flames. I want to touch the flames, feel the fire. Is this the Holy Spirit? Or are these the eternal flames of Hell? Mother lifts her hand. Her wedding ring's diamond mounting rotates the ring on her skinny finger. "God be with you," Father says.

She whimpers a tinny "Thank you." He holds her hand, chalky paper skin, burrowed veins, bony knuckles. She manages a tentative smile and heaves a sigh that trembles her body.

Suddenly I pity her, her life dictated and defined by someone else. Harvey's wife, Harvey's widow, the "little woman," as he called her in his drunken stupors. Forty years at the Credit Union, keeping the family afloat while he drifted from job to job. His binge drunks, the time he fell against the heirloom china cabinet and crushed the door and half the dishes. Her broken arm when she fell down the stairs, if you could believe her. And in the last months, her frustration at his ignoring the doctor's death threats if he veered from his medication regimen. Was there a grin behind her grimace? Did she think good riddance? She must have loved him. Or needed the pain. Or couldn't accept living alone. Who cares? If it's good enough for her, it's good enough for me. At least someone will be praying for him.

"In the name of the Father, and of the Son, and of the Holy Spirit."

"Amen."

Poetry - Betty Hartnett

Haiku 2

dressed in his uniform
from fifty-eight years ago
and now, "Taps"

Broken

Through the ice-edged pane she tracks
her husband's wayward path
as he slogs into knee-deep snow,
trudging toward the barn, head bent,
to slap belts across bovines, latch cups to teats.

She remembers, as she presses their son
into the curves of her swollen breasts,
that this man once loved her,
before the barn and the booze broke him
and snatched away her dreams.

Montana Log Cabin Cafe

buffalo head wall-mount
table three orders
burgers and fries

arrowhead collection
featured assortment
7up, Coke, Sprite, Orange

artifacts,
place settings
for the ancestors

free-range beef
organically raised
on stolen prairie

Poetry - Marilyn Wolff

Budding Author

The mother reads to her little daughter
page after page, chapter after chapter,
book after book.

She did not know that she was
igniting a passion that would fill
page after page, chapter after chapter,
book after book.

We've Had Trouble with This Dog Before

The Animal Control officer comes into my waiting room in the middle of the afternoon. People in the chairs pretend to read, they look at their shoes, fearful, anxious. Nobody likes the dentist. They say, "I hate being here—I hate the dentist!" You don't need to tell me.

I hear a booming voice over the whine of the drill, the gurgling noise of the suction: "I have a warrant!"

I am very busy. I don't need this. You can imagine the nervous people peering over the tops of their magazines.

My receptionist comes back to tell me about the visitor; says he's here about my dog. As if I didn't know. "I'll be right there," I say. The dog's name is Stella—from *A Streetcar Named Desire.* Two years ago, Stella wandered a few blocks from my little house in the country into town, past the city limit. She took up with two town dogs, bad dogs with records. They were reported eating leftover turkey near an overturned trashcan. I bailed her out of the pound: fifty dollars.

The Animal Control man wears a belt from which hang an assortment of weapons and devices: handcuffs, pepper spray, a pistol, cudgel, flashlight, choke collar, leash, car keys, a whistle, hunting knife, corkscrew, radio. This is a person you should be afraid of, not the dentist.

"I'm citing you for letting your dog run loose in the city after repeated verbal warnings!" the officer announces to everyone when I appear in the waiting room. The patients put down their reading.

"Once," I said. "And that was two years ago!"

"Nevertheless," he says, waving the citation, "it's happened again. You need to come with me."

We leave. I follow him to the city courthouse. I pay a one-hundred dollar fine. We drive to the pound. I pay seventy-five dollars for the release of Stella. "If this happens again," the officer says, "the dog will be confiscated!"

"What!" I say. Clearly, he has issues with his teeth, a dark history in the chair.

When I get back to the office, the waiting room has more people in it than when I left. They look up. They smile. I know they have been talking among themselves, but now they are silent.

"My dog is in the car," I say. "It's hot. I need to take her home." Nobody says anything. "I am leaving," I say. "I will be back."

It seems they are willing to wait.

Poetry - Betty Hartnett
Haiku 1

the eagle sits
on a distant bough, waiting
for the grass to move

Censored

Limbs intertwined,
naked as the day they were born,
they lie shamelessly
on the soft rug
in front of the crackling fire.
He cradles her protectively,
one long muscular leg
stretched across
her small, silky soft body.
Gently, he nibbles
her face, neck, and ears.
Eyes closed,
the tip of her pink tongue
teases, touches
his whiskered face.
My dog and my cat are in love.

Open All Night

It isn't what you think—
it never is.

The woman in the pale blue sweats
cradles a warm nightgown;
thinks maybe, just maybe,
she will take down the silver-framed
painting of Eros over her bed.

As he waits for his socks to dry,
the man in the black-slit jacket
looks out the window, wonders
who will drink the single glass
of white wine left on the table tonight.

Each came from a home
with red shutters. Each stood
in ice-blue light. As children,
each asked themselves
if their father loved their mother.

It isn't what you think—
it never is.

A Magnetic Attraction

I ignored Dierdre last winter. Every day she stood at the edge of the water, facing the ocean, in her dingy, white, floppy hat, with magnets belting her waist. I accepted the consensus of my fellow sunbathers—snow birds and locals. "She's a kook."

I listened to the gossip. *She wears the magnets to release toxins from her liver. She and her husband Brian are New Yorkers. They lost their jobs. They left their jobs. Their house is in foreclosure. They live in their car. They live on the beach.* I didn't care.

This year mid-January, I trek down the cliff trail to my favorite island beach, and there she is—standing where I last saw her when I left Kaua'i in April. Incredulous. "Kook" simply can't be the essence of this woman.

I step into the water beside her. "Aloha. You are still here." I introduce myself. "What do you think about standing here gazing at the ocean?"

"Today . . . my mom. I'm missing my mom. She's in her eighties and I haven't seen her for three years."

I expected a discourse on transcendental meditation or Hindu philosophy. The earthiness of her response takes me by surprise. We talk about our mothers. Mine died decades ago, but lives vividly in my memory.

The next afternoon, confident in our bond, I say, "Tell me your story." She obliges.

She's fifty-six. She and Brian have been married twenty-one years. She taught Special Education in a suburban New York City school in the first years of mainstreaming. It was difficult, and her college friends were earning more money and enjoying life in NYC. She escaped the suburbs to work in human resource type jobs in NYC. (I know she isn't fabricating her teaching experience. I served on a school board during the tumultuous 1970s.)

She doesn't fill in the gaps from then to now, nor am I interested in chronology. I'm searching for some nebulous life of the mind.

She does have a unique liver disease. The prognosis isn't good . . . . She's done traditional medicine, alternative medicine, Homeopathy. She learned about the magnets from a woman with the same disease. Magnets and water. Warm ocean water. She's been in Kaua'i a year and a half, but isn't getting better.

"Standing there a year and a half! Stupid," the sunbathers mutter.

Dierdre and Brian rent an old shack in a town nearby where Brian cooks for her and does odd jobs when he can find them. She can't live in the shack. She's chemically sensitive. She must be outside.

"What happens to you in a toxic environment?" I ask.

"Panic attacks. I can't breathe. It's like asthma. No . . . more like a seizure."

She adheres to a rigid daily schedule—five hours standing in the ocean with the waist magnets. This winter she also fastens magnets to a headband beneath the floppy hat—"to make my brain work better, steady my thinking."

Brian spends the night with her in a shelter on the beach, leaves in early morning, brings her breakfast and lunch, and returns at 6 p.m.

"He's a geekie kind of guy, really smart," she says. "He had a successful career in the financial world. He's given up everything for me . . . . He hates it here now."

She can't leave though. She almost died last time she flew.

"What happened?"

"Seizures."

"You're trapped?"

She turns from me to the ocean and nods.

I wander down the beach daily now and stand with her, knee-high in the ocean, facing the horizon. I offer crumbs of my snowbird life in Kaua'i. "I knit . . . cook . . . read piles of books when I'm not at the beach."

"I love to read," she says. A friend, with full-body tattoos and piercings in navel and nipples, brings her books.

"What do you read?" (I expect Maeve Binchy or Barbara Delinsky.)

"*Bee Season* and *Pearl of China* recently. I like Ann Tyler . . . love Mary Oliver's poetry."

I take her two books in a Ziploc, so she can keep them dry. "Thanks so much, but these have been lovingly used . . . remember . . . I'm chemically sensitive." Her tone is always serene, a sharp contrast to my brusque Minnesotan.

This morning she trekked to a cliff clearing where she phoned her mother. She misses her mom. A happy ending to her story, she tells me, would be to see her mom again. That reaches deep into the mother me. I have three daughters.

We turn from mutual mother sadness to books. She surprises me again. "Do you know Marge Piercy's poetry? Brian and I went to a B&B once where she read her poetry during Tea Time."

"Piercy's written novels you might enjoy. She also wrote an excellent book about writing."

"Have you read Stephen King's *On Writing*?" she asks. "Or Natalie Goldberg's?"

(Who are you, Deidre?) "Tell me about this interest in writing."

"I wanted to be a journalist, but my SAT scores were too low for NYU's program. I went to the 92nd Street workshop in NYC once, but the teacher was poetry editor of *The New Yorker*. Intimidating. I never went back."

(I google 92nd Street Y when I get home. Poetry workshops *are* offered there.)

I take her a page of Mary Oliver's poetry, gleaned from Google. We stand together, facing the ocean, our backs to the sunbathers. We're alone in the blue, blue, blue-green to white clouds on the horizon. Accompanied by the bass roar of waves in the distance, the rhythmic splash of waves washing ashore, I read "The Sun." My voice emerges full, deep, calm. The sun, the sky, the sea enclose us. We are one within the words.

It is a spiritual experience. Souls attract in unlikely places.

Who's At the Door?

If death would call ahead
To say he's stopping by
We could tidy up
Dust off our lives

Set out the refreshments
The good dishes
The good deeds
If only we knew

Just look at this mess:
Unfulfilled promises
Unresolved differences
All these plans

We'd set aside time
Where did it go?
Now someone's at the door
Pounding, pounding!

"Surprise!"

When death comes waltzing in
Party hat askew
Intentions litter the floor
Price tags still attached

Poetry - Leane Flynn

Late-Night Subway Song

The world underground was covered in a filthy film
Cloudy, like a gray abstract painting
Layered with smells of salty pretzels and smooth, sweet
       cologne
Inhabited by old, long-toothed rats and piles of rustling
       newspapers

We waited in silence
—thinking of nothing—
For the friendless woman beneath the dark, red cloak
       With hair fresh and woven like an expensive
              tapestry
For her tired, ubiquitous voice to bellow
       swing low—and then—we began to listen—*sweet
              chariot*—
       and later—we began to sway—*carry me home*—
Into the hollow corridor
       Pushing us forward
As the train screamed   and paused   and screamed again

We looked past the fresh dust with reticent smiles
       The crooked melody continued to dance, heated and
              careless
We let it lead us away from the leftover life
       Plastered against the cold concrete station floor
We let it lead us away from the long-felt wait
We let the song coil around our gritty, vacant faces as we
       gazed at our filthy shoes

Sock Drawer

On the littered shoulder of the freeway,
receiving the first needles of a day-long rain,
lay a single, empty drawer. Perhaps

it slipped from a dresser
in an over-loaded pickup or fell
from the square jaw of a garbage truck.

I longed to take the drawer home
and let it contain things again:

>anarchy and stolen cigarettes
>catfights and gym shorts
>eye shadow and iPods
>sisters' secrets.

But it's too late.

Maybe I'll bury
the drawer and let it fill with earth,

or let it hold my dead
daughter's saved socks,

with their worn, grey heels,
slack weave, and bands of blue flowers.

Poetry - Cheryl K Gordon

Addiction

From my heart it comes,
never to be received.
Her darkness grows.
The animal inside snaps and growls—
she doesn't know why.

I watch from the outside;
I hear the train whistle.
I turn away, close my eyes,
and wait for the sound,
knowing I can do nothing more.

Poetry - Margaret M. Marty
Unfinished Business

I see him crawling on hands and knees
with grain to coax the ruffed grouse
that finally dared to eat from his hand
in the quiet snow of winter.

I hear his laughter inside his shop
where he invited baby raccoons to live,
until they hid the pendulum of his clock,
and he had to shoo them away.

A 1955 license plate from his old truck,
the foundation of the barn that burned,
animal drinking cups strewn around,
a metal feed tank, bent awry.

The barbed-wire fence, rusty,
now partly buried in the ground—
I yank and pull, snip it into small pieces
and place it in the trash.

The pile of once new, but now old
fence posts left in the woods
where he cut them for future use,
but never got back to bring them home.

My father's spirit echoes through this heirloom farm.

Cheesecake

The night the squirrel broke through the kitchen screened window and fell into the sink, I had just made a cheesecake. It had been years since I'd made cheesecake. In fact, the last time I'd made this rich concoction, I was single. Like I was now, come to think of it. Surely, I'd made a cheesecake during my marriage . . . but I had no memory of it. The husband I'd signed on with didn't like the way I cooked. Or the way I didn't—perhaps more apt. I believe he would've loved my cheesecake, but I'd become discouraged before that idea ever came to mind. I'd last left off with cooking, before marriage—culinary experiments for my roommate, and the various boyfriends. The cooking that I managed in my married-with-children state included throwbacks to that era: Quiche Lorraine, Spinach-Apple salad. Waffles. Oh, for a fondue pot!

"But, where's the actual dinner?" my husband would invariably ask.

"This *is* the actual dinner," I'd invariably reply. Things went from there to worse. One evening my husband walked in the door from his doctor work, and said, "Hmmm . . . I should just eat at the hospital!"

"Yes!" I said. "Could you?" I plopped our squirming toddler into his arms. "A perfect solution!" He looked aghast.

My mother, concerned about my then-husband's eating status, called each morning—with inspiration. "Poor Jay!" she'd say. "He works sooo hard! Now Shasha—go out and get a nice cut of meat, some potatoes, carrots . . . . Pot roast is so simple. All you have to do is . . . ." Every morning I would get an "all you have to do is" phone call. That's what I called them. I always got stuck at the part that was about how hard Jay worked—and the part of the "all you have to do is" plan that involved leaving the house to procure food items, getting two very young children ready to leave the house, without having to start over too many times.

On occasion, I tried cooking something new—extrapolated from whatever I could find in the cupboards.

"Is this—*pineapple* in the pasta?" Jay said, looking rather baffled.

Not being native to Minnesota, I could use this one: "It's a casserole," I said. "It's just that you're used to 'hotdishes'."

Each night when Jay climbed into bed, he'd say, "What do you have planned for tomorrow's dinner?"

And each night I would say, "I haven't thought that far ahead." Until one night I responded, "Why do you ask me that same question every single ding-dang night?!"

"So we'll know what meat to take out of the freezer," he said.

"*What* freezer?!" I said. You're probably getting the idea. Never mind that one of our children would not, as she described it, eat anything that "involved a fork"—and our four-year-old would not eat any food that, as he put it, "used to walk," thinking to clarify, "Did chocolate chips used to walk?" Lucky for both of us, they did not.

The cheesecake had a gingersnap crust and, true-to-form, I can't follow a recipe. Recipes neglect important pieces of information—when to prepare the Jell-O first, as opposed to just dumping the artificially colored sugar packets straight into the mix. Secondly, ideas come to mind along the way. I had to supplement with Double Stuf Oreos for the crust—and throw in some brown sugar. (It's my long-held belief that brown sugar improves absolutely anything.) All cheese from the refrigerator was needed, even the mozzarella cheese sticks. Seeds from the fresh lemons embedded the ricotta.

Neighbor Sarah and daughter Sophia had dropped by just in time to observe the perfectly smooth cake emerge from the oven—emanating almond scent so sweet that it made our eyes water. Settled at the dining room table, warnings were issued about the lemon seeds. In taking first bites, two things happened at once: everyone said, "*Mmmmm*"—and a deranged squirrel catapulted through the kitchen screen, falling into the sink with a thunk that shook our plates. In split-second unison, we were screeching, leaping, and scattering—like pinballs sprung loose from a vigorous whack. Sarah and Sophia sprinted to the foyer, Lissa dashed upstairs, and Lyric bolted to the hall closet. I shut the door to the study and dialed 911.

It turns out, "squirrel in the house" is not an "appropriate" reason to call 911. I was summarily referred to the yellow pages. "The phone book is in the kitchen," I said, "—with the squirrel."

Suddenly, I recalled "Critter Control"—my lucky discovery the time a stubborn raccoon would not leave our garage. I got the after-hours recording: "If you have a live animal that needs to be removed, press one . . . ."

I offered Lyric five dollars to climb over the back fence and open the door that leads from the kitchen to the side yard, envisioning that the squirrel would choose to walk out the door. I boosted her over the fence. Peering through fence slats, I saw her tiptoeing to the door, opening it— tentatively . . . then running back, full speed, her mouth a big round O. The squirrel was not interested in the exit strategy.

Sarah, with an over-excited Sophia in tow, left— encountering Joe, from a block over, on their way down the alley. In minutes, Joe arrived—gallantly sporting boots and carrying a large net.

While cowering in the dining room, we heard varying *bangings-around*—and all-of-a-sudden, the squirrel was indeed shepherded out the door.

Joe was holding his hand out to greet me, saying something about my lovely house, as I ran into the kitchen, right into his arms—startling him. He looked remarkably like my ex-husband, startling me.

Apparently, Joe told Sarah how nice it had been to see me, again—which puzzled me—I didn't recall having met Joe before. I wondered if I should bake something, to thank him—you never know just what might happen if you experiment with a recipe.

Poetry - Kristin F. Johnson

Snowball's Chance

Shape, press, and knead your snow
as if sculpting the perfect bread roll.
Then pile up the white ammo
round like cannon balls
ready to throw,
perchance at unsuspecting friends.
Save ice balls
for foes.

The Dog

The dog is from another life, so she mustn't write about the dog. The Chesapeake retriever looks up at her from the floor. *Master, who are you? You have changed. Let's go outside.* No. She is going to write serious poems. Like Dorianne Laux, *no sissy poems* for her. No poems about dogs. Yet, she is reminded of the lines from a poem by Deborah Keenan, *the desire for order corrodes the spiritual journey.*

Two days ago, the ex dumped the dog with her: the dog with separation anxiety, arthritis, and a torn ACL in her knee; the dog that used to let the kids ride on her back when everyone was younger. And the dog was stronger. The dog follows her wherever she goes, hobbling from room to room. Last night she couldn't take it. She felt the dog's pain when it yipped, rolled onto its bad leg, and disturbed her peaceful dreams. She missed the puppy from the past that ran and retrieved, dove off the dock into the lake. She called the vet this morning, considered charging the surgery, which might not work anyway. She thought of putting the dog down. The vet reminded her the dog has been living this way for over a year. That's her way: Extreme in her wish for order, fix what's broken or die.

She decides to go outside. The dog trots around the back yard, limping only slightly. The dog lies down, scratches its back on the dew-covered grass with all paws pointing to the sky. Three fat robins hop within four feet of the dog— and the dog doesn't seem to care, doesn't feel the need to run and chase them all away; instead, my retriever pounds her big brown tail against the lawn. When I go to pet her, I notice her black wet nose, her caramel-colored eyes. And then my dog licks me—a big sloppy kiss, that covers half my face.

Retrospection

I want to go back.
I want to see sunshine streaming through dust motes on a
    June morning
And hear kids' voices in the kitchen.
I want to feel the joy of a new day stretched before me
    while my mind races with
creative plans and my fingertips itch to accomplish them.
I want to hear the dog bark to go out and feel the cat
    slither its way inside.
I want to find spilled cornflakes on the table, step on
    dinosaurs in the family room,
paint a picture, and sew new curtains.
I want to watch Huckleberry Hound cartoons on a black
    and white TV and color my
toenails shocking pink.
I want to share coffee and gossip with my neighbor on the
    back stoop.
I want to walk down a sun-dappled sidewalk and, in a herd
    of kids, spot the one on the
psychedelic bike with hair the color of summer wheat.
I want to hear his conversation when he doesn't know I'm
    listening.
I want to drive to the library in a hot car and find new
    books and stillness in its cool
interior.
I want to husk the corn for Sunday dinner at Grandma's and
    plan what dress I'll wear
on Saturday night.
I want to hear the Tijuana Brass and bounce a toddler on
    my lap.
I want to kiss an *owie,* read a bedtime story, and chase
    bears from under the bed.
I want to run my fingers through someone's hair at one in
    the morning and curl into a
warm cocoon beside him.
I want to dance and skip and sing just for the fun of it, but
    there's little energy for
dancing and skipping when you're old.
And not so much to sing about.

Now More Than Ever

I put my face close to hers,
gently touch her hand.
She covers my fingers with hers, smiles,
says softly, "Your hand is cold."

My hands tighten as on prison bars
from the outside, longing that she be free.
I look into her eyes and beg for recognition,
pleading for a sign of our shared memories.

This day is different. I have known days
when my name would light a spark in her eyes.
She would repeat it after me carefully,
"Kate," she'd say, and then "*My* Kate?"

Now more than ever yours, Mother,
now, when I would give all I have
to see the spark again, to tell you
how I love your life and grieve this death.

Down There

Down there I can hear said the boy, the little cousin we lost in the '30s. He had gone swimming with us in the granite quarries and had heard a buzzing. *If I go down deeper* he said in his deaf child's underwater voice, *I'll be able to hear, really hear,* he said as he ran back and dove in again. The quarry was a deep-water place, all hard angles and cold, so very cold, but kids came and swam most every summer day. Most surfaced, but Ben heard a siren's song and stayed. He would have stayed for almost any little bit of sound, but he was sure if he dove deeper there would be more, a hearing world, a host of voices, of frogs nattering, birds with their marvelous songs, his mother's voice. Down there, in the inky cold waters of the quarry was a voice, her voice. The one he lost the day he was born.

Beaten

The vet's office was filled with big banner ads of cardboard cutout dogs that looked like champions and promised your dog would, too. She was offended by the idea that her dog was not already a champion with or without the Science Diet. Her dog was offended by everything, but mostly by the Shih Tzu that growled at him at the door and the cat that thought he was the biggest, most wonderful thing to rub on it had ever seen.

Bear looked forlornly up at her. *If that cat rubs its tail on my head one more time, I'm going to give it something to remember me by.* She pushed the cat away as discreetly as she could with her foot.

The vet said, "Yup, that's probably cancer; it'll be what kills him."

She stared at the man with the huge stomach and tiny feet.

"We like giving these old dogs a good easy end. Now I want you to feed him nothing but the Science Diet out of the can for seniors."

"Seniors?" She looked from the vet to her big, *not* senior dog, both sitting and panting, both with hind legs shaking beneath the strain, Bear because of hip dysplasia, the vet with no excuse.

The vet nodded; he licked his swollen lips. "Oh, yeah, these big old guys are really wonderful. I'll get you a case on your way out but there isn't any reason for surgery or anything like that. Not when they're this old."

Nothing came out of her mouth.

His assistant brought in a case of dog food that she took and held tightly to her chest. Bear kept his head buried in her crotch; he'd had to duck down to that area since he reached his full height seven years ago and, in stressful times like these, she allowed it.

She paid the one hundred and fifty dollar evaluation bill. *So what you're telling me is that you won't get rid of the lump on his chest, that you won't do anything for his hips, that you won't help him in any way, that I am too late except to buy your god damned dog food.*

And she did; she bought the case of dog food and put it in the back of her car. Earlier, Bear had actually convinced her that the drop from her car to the ground was too far for his delicate hips. Now he proceeded to leap into the back seat and vault to the front passenger seat where he sat, tongue hanging out of the side of his mouth, looking positively elated.

"Let that vet see you now." She said it sarcastically but it barely came out. When she sat down, she gripped the steering wheel with both hands. Bear reached over and gummed her right ear and she gritted her teeth against the pain.

Her father had taken their new pup to hunting training when he turned seven months old. Bear was alone, outside, for six weeks in a cement kennel. When they went to pick him up, she had raced down the slope, past the barking dogs, past the boxes of birds for hunting, searching for him. Bear was small then, all big feet and floppy ears. He crept from his kennel, looking over his shoulder, eyes fearful and sharp and she knew then, absolutely, that he had been beaten.

She had fallen to her knees and cried out, held her arms open. Bear had winced at the sound of a human voice; he glanced back at the trainer, moved at a cautious trot that bounced him along. His rough hide was spotted with dirt and burrs. He came toward her because he had been ordered to.

But she was unable to proceed with caution, unable to fathom that maybe he hated humans now, maybe he would lash out at her. She buried her hands in him, unable to stop her fingers from his hard and soft places, from his back and belly and ears. But he did not know her, did not recognize her. He stood with his head close to her face—entirely frozen in fear and confusion even as she rubbed and crooned and begged.

Then she felt his big ribs widen as he took in a breath and Bear gasped. He pushed his nose into her hair, into her neck and ears and face. He trailed every line of her body in disbelief. *Is it really you?* He got into her lap and clasped down on one ear and she held all of his quivering bulk against her heart. *I thought I would never see you again.*

In the car later, her father had sneered, "My stupid dog doesn't even remember us."

Her mouth fell open. She was holding Bear in the back seat to keep him from jumping into the front, into her lap. She said, "Bear is my dog."

Not many years after, Bear was the first thing put in her car when she drove away for good.

They were on the road to another vet office and the rain was coming down in a clingy mist. The humidity made the car claustrophobic and she turned the A/C on high. Bear sat beside her, panting nervously, showing the red droops beneath his big eyes. He kept glancing at her, kept glancing at the road and she glanced at the lump on his chest. It was the size of a fist, had taken six years to get that big. *Cancer, my ass. It's a fatty tumor; it doesn't hurt him. He is not a dog I will allow to slip through my fingers and die choking on Science Diet!*

She needed someone to tell her that they would help him get up easier in the morning. That they would help him chase rabbits and catch chipmunks in the barn. She fisted her hand in Bear's rough hair but there was no fight in that fist because she couldn't get their morning out of her head: after ten minutes of calling and calling for him, Bear had finally showed up at the front door, looking at her quizzically as if to ask, *Why don't you talk to me any more?* He had never heard her and she didn't know if he ever would again.

She looked at his graying face and he gazed back at her. *Can't we just go back home?*

She could see when this would be the last time he fogged up the window, the last time he asked for home. He reached over and gummed her right ear and she wondered where she was going to bury him.

A semi turned the corner and roared by, spraying her little car down with rock and rain, making the seats and the steering wheel quiver. Bear jumped and it scared them both.

Picking Coal

My mother, as a young girl,
scrambles up the side of a railroad bed
scraping knees, grabs pieces of coal
that drop from the train.
Tucked into her smock pockets,
she carries them home,
adds them to her brother's hod.
They hope to have enough
for a few nights warmth.

Back to the tracks they rush
after school each day and wait
with other children for the coal train
to pass the rough crossing.
Boys with blackened hair
turn their hats into bags. Girls
wear old socks on their hands,
fill their aprons, gathered in front
to overflowing, if they are lucky.

The councilmen are horrified
when Tommy Turner, trying to be first
fell beneath the train. His leg is tossed
into the pine box with the rest of his body.

Their solution:
outlaw the gathering of coal.

Returning for a Family Funeral
for Cheryl

Where we returned to doesn't matter,
that we returned to family, and that we returned for a
    funeral, does.

A funeral for Grandma, an aunt, an uncle
would have been understandable; they were old.
But this funeral was for the first of Grandma's twenty
    grandchildren to die.
Cheryl was right in the middle. Ten cousins older and nine
    younger,
next to me, and I remember most, her smile,

like an inverted rainbow.
But she, everyone said, was a true rainbow.

At the funeral, they held afghans she had crocheted;
red, orange, yellow, blue, purple gifts
covered laps, hung across the backs of church pews.

Her siblings had been with her three days earlier,
so she had not been alone with that smile when she died
even though her parents drove around the block and
    around the block—
which corner were they rounding when she took her final
breath? when the coroner stopped?

She smiled when she told me she had bladder cancer, of all
    things—
she who had needed help in the bathroom even at the age
    of seven.
I asked my mother one Christmas Day at Grandma's
why Aunt Marie still went with Cheryl after dinner.
She was six months older than I was,
and I could not remember the last time I needed help.

We have the same brown eyes;
her brown hair has curls; mine is longer, straighter.

103

All my jokes are funny to her; I laugh at her jokes, too.
She walked with a limp.
Stiff braces, heavy brown shoes, no "Mary Janes" for her.
But, she smiled.

Mom says she was scared after Cheryl was born.
If it could happen to her brother's child, it could happen to
      her own.

Cheryl's smile—that's what drew my attention away
from the Spina bifida.
I never saw the hole, the stitched scar on her back.

Her parents should have been there
when she died, seen her smile one more time.

Inside the church that day were rainbow afghans clenched
      in shaking hands,
and rainbows made from sunlight refracted by the tears
      that rolled off our cheeks.

Poetry - Sarah J. Cox
Budapest, October 19, 2011

Peter, a survivor of the Budapest Ghetto
showed us first the monument to Raoul Wallenberg—
a Hercules slaying a snake with a stick.
Earnestly described the work that saved ten thousand Jews.
In an offhand manner he translated the inscription:
Raoul Wallenberg, who saved some people
from death by the Nazis.

I know you can't read Hungarian, he said.
but what word is missing from that inscription?
We stared at him blankly. *Jew,* my friend said.
You're right, he said. *Even on his monument*
they cannot say, he tried to save the Jews.

Then he wanted us to see the shoes. Shoes!
Men's shoes. Women's heels. Children's sandals,
wrought in bronze and copper, fixed in the concrete of the
       bulkhead
on the bank of the Danube, where, in the final hours of the
       war,
young oafish thugs—would-be Nazis—
gathered as many Jews as they could, made them strip,
bound any three together, shot one of the three in the head,
pushed all three into the icy waters. (They were short on
       ammunition.)

Finally, in the Synagogue, Peter took questions.
Is there discrimination now? I asked. *Official or unofficial?*
Listen to me, he said. *There are 386 members in the*
       Hungarian Parliament.
Eighteen of them are actively, openly members of the
       Hungarian Nazi Party.
None of them is a Jew.

Peter went on, then suddenly stopped,
was silent.

I can't talk about this anymore, he said.

Curling Water, Severed Rock
Minneapolis, August 2, 2007

Purple and yellow flowers
clutch the brittle stalks
of prairie grasses
on the banks
of the Mississippi
as it drops smoothly over
St. Anthony Falls, as if
nothing momentous
happened here yesterday,
where it flows through the ruins
of the 35W bridge.
The Dakota call this place
Minirara—curling water.

Divers in rubber suits
sink down into the muddy
river, its rushing
currents, hoping to find
a trace for the families that wait
in the dryness of their grief,
who pace in hotel rooms
provided by the Red Cross.
The Ojibwa call this place
Kakabika—severed rock.

At least two babies in the water;
one torn from the arms of its drowning
mother, the other still
in her watery womb. Up above,
the rescue boats bob about.

In hospitals, limbs in traction,
no-named bodies broken,
and in the deep, the slippery

dead are slipping away.
Sunken words.
Curling water. Severed rock.

The Thrill of Victory

On a fall day in 2006, my doctor announced I had a detached retina. Swimming, a life-time passion, would have to stop to avoid more damage to the eye.

After four years of retirement, I had become familiar with my simple morning rituals. Quiet winter mornings were spent cross-country skiing on the trails near my home, waiting always for that first breath of spring, and the warm weather that would mean I could swim in the lake again. Early summer mornings, when the dew was still on the grass, I would start the pontoon's motor and back away from the dock to cruise along the shore, moving past the mother ducks with their trail of babies and the Blue Herons pretending to be statues. Speeding up, I would circle the lake to stop in the middle and descend the ladder, pushing off the last step to glide on my back, floating as I stared up at the sky. The water surrounded me with its liquid embrace. The lake and I were one as I lay suspended on its surface. But now, with my doctor's words, all of this would change.

After my diagnosis, many surgeries and treatments followed in hopes of saving my sight. Slowly I lost complete vision in my right eye. Then, the crushing news that the left retina had also detached. Soon all vision was gone with only perception of light left to guide me.

I could no longer drive or read or look at the sweet faces of those I loved. I keened in grief and raged in anger. How was I ever going to survive this? How was I to continue without the ability to do the things I loved?

While I grieved my losses, it was finally time to move on to restore the things in my life that sustained me. Through the National Library Service, I received books on tape. Minnesota Services for the Blind gave me computer training and I learned to type, thanks to a talking program. They also provided white cane training to guide my walking. You wouldn't believe the number of talking devices which give me independence—talking clocks, a talking kitchen timer, and even a talking scale. All of these things improved my standard of living as a blind person.

There were many facets of my life I had to reclaim. But to gain the essence of my former life with vision, I wanted to swim again, to feel the water envelop my body with its silky liquid. And that blessing was yet to come.

In November, 2010, a new friend, a former swimming coach, offered to help me. And so we began our days as a swim team—Pat the coach and Nancy the blind swimmer. Pat led me to the edge of the pool and coached me down the three steps into the cold water. I submerged my whole body to once again feel the water's embrace. After a five year absence, I had returned, the water as familiar as my own home. But we soon encountered a problem. Without sight, I had no point of orientation and bumped into either the side of the pool or the lane line rope. This kept Pat on alert to shout, "Go right!" or "Go left!" as I zigzagged down the lane. After several sessions of this, we thought, "Is this going to be our defeat? How can we make progress under these conditions?"

We left the pool that day unusually quiet. I felt defeated and wondered if I could continue. What could I do to stay in my lane and swim in a straight line?

Discussing this problem with my engineer husband, Neil, we came up with the concept of a string line hooked at each end of the pool and a belt around my waist to tether me to the line. After a few tries, Neil was satisfied with the results.

At the pool, I grasped the line over my shoulder, its tension biting into my palms as Pat tied the knots. Now the big question—would it work? Pat said, "Go for it!" I turned, facing the lane and laid into the water, swimming the sidestroke. I could feel the line as I neared the end. I made it! Turning around, I headed for the other end, feeling the line over my shoulder, right on course. As I climbed out of the pool, Pat was there, clapping with joy.

Later, we left the locker room, our heads together in animated conversation, chattering about our day's success. I tucked my arm into Pat's, my white cane searching ahead. Now we were a real swim team.

As we stepped outside the school door, it had begun to snow. We lifted our heads to feel the kiss of wet snowflakes on our faces. It didn't matter what struggles were before me; I was finally back. Oh, to be alive! To feel the thrill of victory!

The Same Stars

I am
so far from home,
so far from everything
that is safe and secure.

what a relief
to look up to the night sky,
to see the familiar faces of the stars,
the same constellations,
the same sky.

I am not lost
after all.

Ice Talk

Listen
to rare lake sounds
of water and ice performing
a ghostly ancient
pipe organ song
echoing under the surface
as in a hall of a glass cathedral.
The lake's flowing voice
yields primeval fluid moanings
of phantom whales,
rolling in a crescendo wave,
cascading low tones reverberate
then drift into silence.
The lake sings remembrance
of wails of loons,
fascinating, ethereal—
one end of the lake sings
and the far bay answers
I watch the flat solid surface
and wait in frozen silence
to hear more mysteries
of water making ice.

The Bride

Icy waves crash against large rocks that jut from the lakeshore. A huge cargo ship bellows its horn into the stormy sunset, demanding the lift bridge move out of its way. White birds fight the wind and scream their defiance while large purple clouds chase each other across the darkening sky.

In the safety of the harbor, the waves have settled to small ripples that lap at glistening pebbles. The bay is calm now that the tempest has passed. Crowds of people will soon dot its shoreline but, for now, only one person has dared to brave the fury of the great lake.

The beach is cold under her bare feet, the wind frigid through her long, white dress, the faint sunlight glittering against a lonely diamond ring on her finger. She ignores the billowing cloud of black smoke rising from the trees behind her and stares out into the lake. Sirens howl in the distance, shrieking ever closer. Someone is yelling her name—"Carolina? Carolina!"—as a small smile settles onto her face.

Her hands rise from her sides, embracing the wind that races off the lake like a dance partner. "Would you dance with me, Ray?" she whispers, closing her eyes. Her hips sway back and forth to the rhythm of the waves.

Slowly and gently, she twirls around in circles on the beach. The wind catches at her dirty white dress, wrapping it around her legs. Carolina pushes her long, black hair out of her eyes and tips her head to the side, almost like she was resting it against a shoulder. A wisp of feathery gauze brushes her face.

"Carolina, answer me!"

She freezes in place. Her polished fingernails drop from their dancing position as her shoulders tense. Brown eyes open and glare towards the trees. The smile vanishes from her face, replaced by something dark and shadowed. Her fingers curl into fists by her sides. Smoke from the fire beyond the trees burns acrid in her nose. She starts to tremble.

The sirens are so close they cover the comforting sounds of the waves. Her hands come up to cover her ears, a whine coming from her throat. Suddenly, the wailing sirens cut off, leaving a pressing silence. "Please," she murmurs into the stillness. "Please, Ray, come back."

A wave crashes on the beach. The wind whispers through her hair, brushing it away from her face like the loving fingers of a husband-to-be.

She turns around slowly. As she walks closer to the lake, the shadows on her face vanish and tension flows from her body. A long, slow breath works its way out of her as she crouches on the cold pebbles, close enough for the frigid water to touch her toes. She plays with her engagement ring, turning it around and around on her finger, and watches the lonely ship still making its way into the harbor.

"Ray?"

A dove answers her plea with a mournful cry. A few short beams of light, the very last of the day, cascade through the sky to touch her face. The light collects on the clouds, illuminating their curious shapes and shadows against the approaching blackness.

"That's a stratus cloud," the wind sighs into her ear, just like Ray did when they used to lie on the beach together. Her eyes open slightly, looking to see if she could find the cloud in question. "And that one over there? It's a cumulonimbus."

"That's not a cumu . . ." she trails off, stumbling over the name she'd never been able to pronounce. The waves whisper a laugh against the beach. "It looks like a rabbit. A big, black rabbit."

Silence falls as she waits for Ray to reply.

"Carolina."

A shadow falls over the woman, blocking the meager sun from her face. Carolina turns her head away, keeping her eyes closed. A quiet, soft hum starts up in the back of her throat.

"Carolina, open your eyes." The voice is too loud to be ignored.

Slowly, Carolina opens her brown eyes to stare at the form of her mother. Standing with fists on hips, she has wavy hair that dances with white and a mole on her cheek. Great clouds of black smoke, flickering with oranges and reds and yellows from the flames, rise behind her.

Carolina sits quietly, waiting, running her hands over the soft satin of her once-pristine dress. Her fingers tease and dance at several of the stains that mar the beautiful, snowy color. The wispy veil tucked into her hair blows into her face.

Anger vanishes from her mother's face. "Oh, Carolina, not again." She sighs, shakes her head and stoops, quietly taking the veil out of Carolina's hair. "I've got to hide this dress better." The veil flutters wildly in her mother's hands, trying to get free. When a larger-than-usual wave rushes the beach, her mother takes a few steps back in order to not get wet. Carolina doesn't move. "How come you set all your presents on fire?"

"I'm not getting married," she whispers. "What do I get presents for?"

"The flames set that old apple tree on fire. You're lucky it didn't spread to the house."

Carolina shrugs and looks away, watching the waves lap softly against the shore. The last vestiges of the sun disappear, staining the sky a dark purple. The lake swirls comfortingly against her numb toes.

Her mother lets out a slow breath, closing her eyes for a moment. "You need to stop doing this, sweetheart," she says, taking Carolina's hand and helping her to her feet. "It's been three weeks."

The hem of Carolina's wedding dress dabbles in the water. She gazes out over the lake, watching the water churn and move, and her mother starts to pull her up the beach. "Ray . . ." she breathes.

A wave curls up against the pebbles like a hand reaching for Carolina's foot. It fells just short of its goal.

"Carolina," her mother says, turning the younger woman to face her. She pushes the long hair out of Carolina's face. "Sweetheart. He's not out there anymore."

Carolina cranes her head around, searching the lake's dark waves. "But—"

"No one can survive this long in that lake. He's not coming back, you have to accept that." Carolina shakes her head, but her mother just holds her close and whispers, "Now come along. We've got to get you out of that dress."

Out in the harbor, the ship starts to vanish around a point and a few lonely birds fight their way to the safety of the shore for the night. Waves roar as they slam into the largest of the rocks outside the protection of the bay. There's the sound of voices from the firefighters, working to keep the fire contained to the apple tree.

Carolina stays still, listening and watching, before finally nodding her head and allowing her mother to tow her away from the great lake and the love trapped within its icy depths.

The Silver Screen Shimmers

The silver screen shimmers
Tired eyelids flutter
countering the apple breeze
syncopating
the one-two creak
of the rocking chair
releasing its age

In a fairytale feint
the silver screen shivers
Fingertips brush
the weeping bride's cheek
a catered caress
innocence beckons the groom
illusions end

then resume
In an attic's musty twilight
the silver screen shakes
Forgotten books are found
yellowed leaves caressed
releasing the marbled mix of
dew and musk
from each unveiled page

Sated eyelids lull
glare into shade
shade into shadow
shadow into dusk
as the rocking chair rests
And the silver screen shimmers
shivers and locks
shakes into silence
and the silver screen stops

Love of Water

I wanted to tell
how the water purls
where the stones
lace the skirts
of a stream,
how the turning
of it twines upon
itself and then
      untwines.
I wanted to mouth
the words that say
how the bay tongues
the shore beyond.
But all I could say was
      ohhh . . .

Evel Knievel

As sailboats skim soundlessly over sparkling waters, Husband, Son, and I enjoy lunch on the patio of a dockside restaurant. This is our last family weekend before sending Son off to college.

"How fun would *that* be?" Son gestures toward a moped whizzing down the street. His tone says e*xtremely cool.*

I am drinking my fourth glass of sweetened iced tea and am up for anything.

"I'm in," I proclaim, punching the air with my fist.

"Are you sure you can handle a moped?" Husband asks with trepidation.

"Why not?" I protest, waving my arm expansively. "Look at all these people zipping around. If they can do it, why can't I? How hard can it be? It's not like it's a motor-cycle."

Husband and Son exchange glances.

"Well, Mom, it's just that you have . . . balance issues." This is Son's diplomatic way of saying *Mom, you're a klutz.*

I am a bit piqued. I am competent. I am capable. I am Woman, hear me roar. "Oh, for heaven's sake. If you can do it, I can do it. Let's pay the bill and walk over there."

Son shrugs. Husband shakes his head. They fold.

We stroll into Wheels to Go, where a tanned, bottle-blonde young man is working behind the counter. Brushing a lock from his eyes, he says, "Hey."

"Hey," I reply. "How much does it cost to rent a moped?"

"Twenty-five dollars for the first hour, twenty dollars an hour after that. How long do you want to go out for?"

"An hour, maybe two," I answer. Husband gives a tentative nod.

The young man hands us papers to sign, Son grins, and we adjust the straps on our helmets as we file outside.

"These are Vespas," Bottle-Blonde Boy says seriously. "As the contract states, you are responsible for any damages."

Obviously bored with having repeated the operating instructions too many times, he rattles them off without pause. "This key turns the engine on now this seems backwards to most people but you turn this hand grip toward you to accelerate and away from you to slow down the brake is this handle on the left if you want to store your water bottles turn the key and push and the seat will pop up you can practice in the empty parking lot next door if you want have a nice ride." And he walked away.

Baffled by this litany, I surreptitiously watch Husband and Son and do what they do. Get on the bike, grip the brake with the left hand, turn the key, place right hand on the grip that controls the speed. Revolving it away from me, I kill the engine. Turn key again, twist grip the other way, lurch forward with a smile. *This isn't so hard. Where does Husband get off, asking me if I can handle it?*

Turning into the practice lot, I make a couple of laps. Confidence building, I weave in and out among objects scattered at random on the asphalt. This is obviously an obstacle course intended for practicing maneuvers. Later I learn it is a bunch of junk left behind by skateboarders.

I am startled to see how close I am to the far edge of the parking lot, where a steep embankment plummets, and treetops are almost level with the pavement. I have fifteen feet, maybe less, to make a sharp turn. Although I pull hard to the left on the handlebar, the bike continues to race straight ahead. Note to self: *Vespas do not make sharp turns.*

My eyes pop open like a big fish. In fear, I freeze and tighten my grip on the handlebars, effectively gunning the engine. The asphalt disappears beneath me. *Oh my gosh, I'm going over the edge!*

Sprawled in the scratchy brush, I spit dirt and push weeds out of my eyes. Feeling stunned and ridiculous, I demand of the Woman Who Roars, *How in the world did I wind up here?*

I do a quick body scan. My arms extend straight out in front of me. No problem there. The handlebars of the bike are jabbing me in the pelvis. *Am I broken? I don't think so.* My neck took a jolt, but it feels okay. My legs, however, are pinned. I wiggle the left one free, but the bike lies heavily on top of the other. I cannot move.

"Help! Help! Help!" I am desperately hoping Husband and Son are still doing laps around the parking lot. No response.

I yell louder. "Help! Help! Help! Help!" Still no response. *Don't panic,* I tell myself. *Yell louder.* I bellow like an animal in pain, because now, I am. A voice echoes above the ravine, sounding a long way off.

"Wheerrre aaarrrree youuu?"

"Get this bike off my leg!" I'm shrieking as hard as I can now.

This time, results. Husband peers over the edge of the embankment. "How the heck did you get down there? Are you hurt? Is your leg broken?" He chooses this time to make conversation.

"Get this bike off me!" I scream. "It's heavy and it hurts. Hurry up!"

Husband picks his way down the bank. Grunting and straining, he drags the bike off.

"Thank you so much," I manage politely, rubbing my sore leg.

He gapes at me. "Are you sure you're not hurt? How could you possibly *not* be hurt? You went off the edge! Do you think anything is broken?"

"I think I'm okay. Nothing feels broken. I even think my neck is okay."

He stares at me in disbelief. "Your neck is okay?"

"I really think it is."

Husband's eyebrows are up under his hairline, his cheeks blanched. Thirty-four years ago, I severely injured my neck in a car accident, and it is my weak link. Husband grabs my hand, pulls me to my feet, and we start up the steep bank.

Son is standing at the top, panicky. "Are you hurt, Mom?"

"No, I seem to be fine," I giggle. Then I laugh. Then I double over laughing.

Son comments that if I'm laughing, I must be okay, and he starts snapping pictures. They leave me in the parking lot in a fit of hysterical relief while they tug the bike out of the ravine. It lays ten, maybe fifteen feet down the embankment in a tangle of brush.

After a few minutes, they succeed in hauling the bike back to the top. Laughing again at the image of this, I climb back on the bike and say, "Let's go."

"You aren't serious," Husband says.

"Mom, it's leaking," Son says.

I am not about to be left behind and out of the fun. "I will drive back to the shop and have it checked out. Don't worry. I know how to go forward."

Son and Husband shake their heads and follow me.

Blonde Boy looks the bike over and says, "No problems. You're good to go."

My men are more skeptical.

"Are you sure you want to do this, Mom?"

"Are you crazy?" asks the other.

"Look, I know how to go straight. Now that I know this thing doesn't turn like a bicycle, I'm sure everything will be fine."

The clock is ticking. Time is money. Arguing burns time and money. Husband understands this, so off we go.

Feeling unsteady, I recall Son's comment about my "balance issues." I extend my legs straight out to the sides to catch myself if need be. *Oh, the screaming behind me.*

"Pleeeaase put your feet on the bike! Please! You'll catch your foot and break a legggg . . . ."

I whirr off, gingerly placing my feet on those little shelves on the sides of the bike. *Balance. Focus. How hard can it be?*

I am not smiling, although the wind is blowing my hair and all that. I am concentrating hard, because I see a turn in the road ahead. *I can do this. Nice and easy. Make a wide arc.*

"For God's sake, get over! You're on the wrong side of the highway!" yells Husband. *I can see that. He is all fussed up because my turn is a bit wide.*

Cautiously, I lean to the right. I am getting the hang of it. I am back on the right side of the road. I am proud, and I roar almost as loud as the engine.

The rest of the afternoon passes without further incident, except one close call when a family steps right out in front of me to cross a parking lot. "Watch out for me," I holler. "I'm not that good at this!"

The woman and the girl smile as I career past them, and jump out of the way. The man shouts angrily, "*You* should be watching out for *us*!" He may be saying something more, but I can't hear it over the growl of the engine as I speed away.

Back at the bike shop, I hand over my credit card to a pretty cashier wearing short shorts, a bikini top and flip flops.

"Did you have a nice ride?" She smiles.

"You know, I really did, except the part where the bike zoomed off an embankment and crashed in the bushes."

She slides her eyes sideways and looks at me.

I ignore her, and roar.

Couldn't Be Helped

He's a professor of English
in his day job, but he dreams
poetry at night. Even in class
he's always watching for cues
to launch him into poetic reverie,
like the pretty coed in the front row
who wears insanely short skirts
and keeps crossing her legs
during his lectures, as though
inviting him for a garden stroll.
Instead he meanders down
the stuffy halls of academia,
crossing T's and dotting I's.
So how could it be helped when
the topic of gardening came up
he spelled it *orgasmic* gardening.

Just As Good, and Free

If you'd like to talk to a representative, dial three.
And so I do, but then I'm told to reconsider—
automated is as good, and after all, it's free.

She says my satisfaction is their goal, but who's this *we*?
—a distant techno talker, a lowly head-setted kidder,
saying if you'd like to talk to a representative, dial three?

I want help, now, and would gladly pay a fee.
Instead, I get a drone, some robot telesitter
suggesting automated is as good, and better yet, it's free.

Just give me a live person, a simple answer please—
don't jack around and falsely sooth with electro language
        litter,
lying about that representative, mine by dialing three.

A little compassion, really, that's the key—
not a list of pointless choices, this annoying binary twitter
insisting autoservice is as good, and after all, quite free.

What non-service—mechanical and hollow, clueless as can
        be!
—a who or which that interrupts, a cyberspace pinch
        hitter,
claiming that a human is available by merely dialing three,
though automated is as good, and truly Sir, it's free.

When I Go Sketching in the Woods

dedicated to Mom

When I go sketching in the woods
I want to put it all on the page.
Every green pine bough,
each twisty oak branch,
the lichen-covered rocks,
the fields of emerald fern,
the bald eagle across the river,
the brown beetle scuttling across the path,
the sapphire blue sky pouring through lacy branches.
The job of the artist is to
grow deaf eyes to abundance,
and then bear your focus on that
little bit of bark in front of you
and infuse it with all the love
you have for everything else.

From New York City to New York Mills

It is morning here in rural Minnesota. Like most mornings before it snows, I take Meadow, my yellow Labrador Retriever, for a walk down the gravel road. Actually, I walk myself; the dog is my excuse to forget that I am walking to sidestep the tendrils of melancholy that wrap around my limbs when they are at rest.

The gentle breeze pulls at the warmth from my body, taking away the last skin-sense of Chris, warm and snoring, next to me in the bed. I am alone here.

My legs find a rhythm. Meadow bounds from one side of me to the other. My steps are slow as I unravel the tangle of white rubber earphones, plug them into my iPhone and select a recent "This American Life" podcast to listen to. The left earphone dangles free from the one in my right ear so I can leave my left ear open to the sounds of nature around me. The podcast is about police corruption in New York City. In my right ear, I hear the recorded sounds of car horns and traffic. In my left ear, I hear the chuckle-call of the Sandhill cranes that live in the fields to the north.

Trying to bridge the distance between my two lives is like trying to see two different images at the same time through those old plastic trick toy projectors, each eye-tube leading to a different photograph. When my brain finally puts the left and right images together, a third image, a different image, emerges from the other two.

In my old life in New York City, I woke to the sounds of trucks grumbling at idle at the stoplight outside my window. The air was thick with diesel fumes and the smell of cumin and cooked meat from Pacifico, the upscale Mexican restaurant across the street. Only a thin slice of sky was visible at the top of my window.

Today the sky is covered in soft gray blankets. There is a small opening to the east where a pink sun shines, a crack of morning light visible from beneath cosmic bed sheets. The air is heavy and thick with the promise of rain, comfortable as a robe. A very fragrant robe. Scents of earth, pine and sweetgrass mix into perfume—grassy, earthy, bright and sweet. I inhale soil, trees, and grass.

In New York City, I walked purposefully to the subway over a vector that accommodated crowds of pedestrians in a practiced dance. Along four blocks I passed eight restaurants, four boutiques, the Dominican bodega, the gourmet grocery, and the Korean deli. Sometimes I stopped to buy breakfast. Then, I continued walking while drinking a fruit smoothie from my right hand, tang of fresh pineapple on my tongue. A just-baked scone, yeasty and sweet, warmed my left hand through a transparent slip of wax paper.

Meadow and I have walked the equivalent of four Brooklyn blocks, and we are not even halfway down my driveway. We approach the bend where the driveway turns sixty degrees toward the road. We are now out of sight of my house. My sneakers kick up a sandy, mineral scent off the surface of the gravel driveway. My heart-rate picks up. Meadow and I pass through a field of mixed grasses, wildflowers, and thistles. Clumps of thorny mountain-ash line the driveway to the right. A wire and wood fence parallels the driveway a few feet to my left separating my thin strip of driveway from my farmer-neighbor's field. I pass a deer stand, a hunter's tinker-toy of wood planks nailed together and balanced on stilts in the middle of the field.

In one ear, I hear Ira Glass's voice telling me the story of a policeman in handcuffs. In the other, a splash. Meadow has leaped into a reedy pond of standing water.

This is how I live now: my old world nested into my new one. One ear attuned to the land around me, the other listening back to the city I left.

We exit the tree-corridor and enter my favorite stretch of road. It is wide open on both sides. Fields upon fields of low-lying plants punctuated by marsh. It starts with a short stretch of neatly planted rows of corn, as orderly as the blocks of apartment buildings that sprout up on the Upper West side of New York City. From the field, the land opens up into vastness: nature's full glory of earth and plant and sky. A grass-imbued breeze tousles my hair. The fresh scent of turned-over earth rises from the ditch.

Sometimes, in the glory of the emptiness around me, I can believe I have come home.

Poetry - Patricia Conner

A Bird Flew into my Garden

Landed on my willow tree.
Much like the Firebird of Russian lore
or a bird embroidered out of myth

in tapestries; the silken threads
of her exotic plumage shimmered
dark red, iridescent green, and blue:

When she trilled the coloratura "Bell Song"
from *Lakme,* liquid notes leaping high
into the branches, the leaves were breathless.

Immediately, with a twinkle in her eye,
she shifted down to mezzo, sang the airs
of Cherubino, that naughty boy from *Figaro.*

Until she softened to bel canto: Cio-Cio-San,
lifting in pathos "Un Bel Di," that song of hope
defying absolute hopelessness.

And finally contralto: depth, strength, comfort
hummed beside a cradle, soared to holy rafters,
offered chorally on marches to freedom.

I baked her honey cakes; I brought her berries,
offered shaggy full heads of sunflower seeds.
How could I keep her singing? She repeated *Butterfly*:

"One Fine Day"—the longing trembled in her throat,
began to shake the tree. She soared into the sky
and coasted down in wide concentric arcs,

then smaller, far away. I bowed my head,
stepped back from possession, consoled
my weeping willow tree, and watched her fly.

127

Canticle

The distant "whump"
of a Winchester at first light,
somewhere drakes

windmilling out of the

air trailing
lead shot and down;
on this lake

where the shore breeze scrolls

the belly of the
bay into dissolving ripples a lone goose
dabbles in the shallows, the sky muted pinky

grey by a row of flat clouds banked

along the horizon, the trees at the edge
stand side by side in a brilliantine
display of ochre and umber and

sienna; just now the racy whisper of four

bluebills flying to a pond across the road
comes through the pines.
The goose steps

onto a rim of orange needles

thickening the damp sand and one
useless black webbed foot juts askew,
the long set wound of an ancient victim.

Steaks for Dinner

Shopping carts crashed against each other, and the store loudspeakers boomed music interrupted by an occasional call for a bagger. My husband Bill abandoned his chore of pushing our cart and left me with the shopping. He disappeared into the aisles until I found him at the meat counter.

"I feel like sirloins this week," he said, as he surveyed the beef.

"The doctor said you should have the leanest of cuts," I reminded him.

Ignoring me, he continued, "I like the marbling in this one, although this package has three pieces. That would leave one for me while you're at church bingo. What do you think?"

"Neither looks lean to me."

His arm encircled my waist and squeezed gently, "You're always thinking of me. Here, I got these for you." From behind his back, he presented me with three pink roses. "I found these at the checkout, and they reminded me of our wedding. You were the prettiest bride." He winked, leaned in, and placed on my lips a kiss that tasted of pizza samples.

"Okay, three not-so-lean sirloins."

One week it was pink roses; the next, a bunch of daffodils; another week a bouquet of daisies. For more than thirty years, Bill put flowers in our cart, reminding me of special times in our life—roses at our wedding, daisies like the ones on the hillside where we had a picnic, or a single tulip in celebration of spring; I loved his romantic touches.

It had been a year since Bill's funeral. My shopping habits changed—instead of a gallon of milk, I would take a half-gallon, a pint of cottage cheese, not a quart. Each time I chose the smaller quantity, I was reminded of Bill.

The meat department created the most sentiment. With a painful yearning in my heart, I stood looking at the choices and could almost sense Bill's presence.

As I scanned the selections, a tall, burly man in a red windbreaker wheeled his cart next to mine and said, "Aren't you the new pianist at First Emmanuel?"

"Yes, Pastor Raymond asked me to substitute while Mrs. Donaldson recuperates from surgery. My name is Annie. And you're an usher, right?"

"Yup, my name's Adam Felton. Nice to meet you." He glanced at the meats. "This market sure has expensive meat. Look at these prices," he exclaimed. "I love steaks, but the chicken would be cheaper."

"My husband loved his steaks, too," I said, as I took a single-serving package from the display. "He passed on a year ago, and every time I come to this store, I'm reminded of his passion for food."

Adam looked at my watering eyes. "I'm sorry. It's just that some of these cuts are so high priced."

"Splurge a little. Buy yourself the steaks and savor them." I tried to sound convincing as the memories of Bill returned.

He hesitated, looked at me with a smile. "But they're too costly. I'd better not," and he wheeled down the aisle.

I continued shopping, choosing small cans and packages of food, just enough for me. As I neared the checkout, Adam came toward me. "Here, this is for you," he said, as he handed a bundle of white tissue paper to me; a lone pink rose nestled in its folds. "Pink was my Tina's favorite color. Her wedding dress was pink, and she insisted the men wear pink shirts. She passed away a few years ago."

As the tears welled in my eyes and my lips quivered, I tried to find the right words. This stranger was resurrecting strong feelings, and I wanted to tell him how much I appreciated the touching gift. As I searched for a simple thank you, he wished me a good day, turned, and pushed his cart down the aisle.

I stood there staring at the rose, fending off the tears. Bill's years of buying flowers for me at the grocery had left a deep impression, and now a stranger was reviving those wonderful moments.

While I placed my groceries on the checkout counter, a shopping cart pushed against my backside. "Hi again," a voice behind me teased. I turned and saw Adam. "I took your advice and splurged. See? I got some steaks. I was wondering if you'd care to join me for dinner. I'm well known for my grilling expertise and, if I dare say, I make a mean Caesar salad."

It's been two years and many steak dinners since that memorable day. Adam and I buy groceries together, are still involved at church, and enjoy many of the same things. His refreshing sense of humor and uplifting smile is dulled only by my suggestion that the men wear pink at our wedding.

Blind

Dead a little over a year now, you appear to me at night while I'm asleep. These last few visits frightened me, arriving naked and removing my clothes under the blankets. Then, we're in warm ocean water up to our necks. We are pressed together, your olive skin uncomfortably close—and welcome. You smile with your bedroom eyes half-closed and kiss me. Shaking, I return the kiss, then push you away. My wife is lying beside us; I can't do this with another woman. You and I were co-workers, friends to a degree. My inner desire for you was pure animal; shared sweat on chests, groans from deep in the belly, the bedroom filling with pungent perfume. But you've been dead over a year now and my soul mate is lying next to me, yet you are naked, offering yourself to me under these covers. Between the real and the dream, I silently want this to stop. My wife will wake and catch me dreaming of you. I did desire you, but not now, not this way. The following morning I confess this dream of the other woman to my wife; I've somehow cheated on her. She says it's only a dream, don't be silly, don't worry. Her words rest easy with me for the day. The new night approaches, the full moon shines through our bedroom window. We kiss goodnight. It's quiet. I am restless so I close the blind to block the gazing eye in the clear night sky.

Waking

Silently sliding solo
exposing herself
in the clear crisp
starless sky

slowly slinking
behind pine boughs
hiding peeking and teasing
pulling persistently pulling
to her as she
fades into the dawn

quarter moon hangs low.

Childless

sister, niece—
you two have your own circle
you will not let me in
and I have no right to be jealous of that

mother, daughter—
closer than thought
together every day
finishing each other's sentences
two soul mates if such things exist

childless
I stand outside their circle
the circle they don't even see

The Day I Laughed at a Funeral

It was in September. I should have been in school, but was allowed to miss classes all day to attend the funeral. Kids who were in school would have loved to be off because it was a mild, sunny day, the kind that drives you nuts to be inside because all too soon winter's howling winds and snow would arrive. Even knowing that, I would have preferred to be stuck in Biology or English or Math.

I'd been apprehensive about going to the funeral for several reasons. The fact it was a funeral was number one. It was only the second funeral I'd ever attended in my life; the first had been that of my mother six years before. That experience alone had been traumatic at eight years old. The fact I thought I was mature at fourteen didn't make going this time any easier. When my grandma had passed away just a few months previous to this autumn day, I couldn't bear to go to the church. I mourned alone, sitting in the kitchen at the farm while everyone else attended her services.

Now, mere months later, I was at the small, white church. The second reason I didn't want to be there? The funeral was for my grandpa. After Grandma died, Grandpa had lost his zest for life. It was said then, and still believed years later, that Grandpa died of a broken heart, pure and simple. After having spent fifty plus years together, one couldn't go on without the other.

Back on that September day, I sat on a polished wooden pew two rows from the front, left-hand side. I don't remember who I was next to, probably my sister. What I do remember is sitting on the end of the pew nearest the window. Sunshine was pouring right on me, strong and steady. Dust motes floated in the air. I remember feeling the warmth of the sun even though my insides felt cold and how I couldn't sing "How Great Thou Art" with the rest of the congregation. It was a song I loved, but singing it at my grandfather's funeral when the sun was shining just seemed wrong. It shouldn't have been that way. I cried instead.

Grandpa had been a farmer and lived through the woods behind our house. The farm was my favorite place to go. I loved the big white house with the red porch, the woodstove in the kitchen, the cold milk always available in the tin pitcher in the fridge, and the barn. Whenever I asked, Grandpa would take me for a tractor ride. Even though I was fourteen and my interests were friends and boys and movies and phone calls, the farm was still beloved.

When the services were over, everyone trooped down the stairs to the dining area in the church's basement. The Lutheran ladies had prepared a light lunch of tuna salad, egg salad and ham salad sandwiches on white, wheat and rye bread. The sandwiches were cut diagonally in triangles and arranged neatly on serving trays. Going through the lunch line, there was also gelatin salad, cheese and crackers, and the requisite array of bars and cakes. Whenever there was a funeral or a shower or some sort of event, the call went out to the ladies of the church. They responded. They baked and brought and helped out. At the end of the serving line were cups of red Kool-Aid for the kids, and silver coffee urns with steam wafting from their spouts. This was a primarily Finnish community; of course there was strong, hot coffee.

The atmosphere was somber; why wouldn't it be? It was a funeral. The adults found places to sit at the tables and visited among themselves. My cousins and I didn't want to be with the adults; we traipsed to an empty Sunday school classroom with our plates and sat on the folding chairs.

I remember we quietly picked at our food. No one was really hungry; sadness erased hunger. We'd all loved our grandpa and spent a lot of time together at the farm. We knew that with him gone, and Grandma before him, it was not going to ever be the same.

Then one of the cousins said *Hey, remember when we were all on the hay wagon and the wheel broke, and Grandpa swore?* The cousin imitated Grandpa: "Oh, sit." Grandpa was 100% Finnish and, with his accent, it came out "Oh, sit" and not anything worse. Besides, none of us had ever heard him swear.

We kind of giggled. Then stopped. We looked at one another. Giggling? Wasn't it bad to giggle when we'd just seen Grandpa's coffin lowered in the grave?

Then we talked some more and shared other stories about naming calves, going for tractor rides, staying overnight and the Saturdays when our families would all gather at the farm because we knew the sauna would be hot. We actually laughed a couple of times as we talked.

It was an adult revelation, sort of an epiphany, that we weren't being bad. We were talking about memories and good times and celebrating the life that our grandpa had lived. We knew we were lucky to have had such a wonderful place to go, and had fabulous grandparents. They were gone now but we knew even though we were sad, it was okay to cherish the memories. So on that September day, as a few of us cousins sat in the Sunday school room, we allowed ourselves to laugh. Grandpa had been a happy, contented family man. We figured he'd have approved.

Blueberry Woods Symphony

We packed homemade bread,
a crock of butter, a stick of summer sausage,
a jar of pickled herring, a sack of sugar cubes,
cups from the cupboard and a knife from the drawer.
We filled blue Mason jars, some with water,
others with coffee whitened with cream.
By noon, the water would be warmish,
the coffee lukewarm—a small price to pay
for a day in the blueberry woods.

In forest undercover, berries of powdery blue
grew with those yet pale green and purple.
Children mastered the art of coaxing only
ripe berries off a branch while claiming
frequent tastes of the tangy treasures.
Parents, aunts, uncles, cousins and siblings,
watched over by a crowd of curious crows,
orchestrated a blueberry woods symphony.
Light plinking followed by deep plunking,
then a muted melody as pails began to fill.

Of childhood summers of barefoot freedom,
I recall nothing with greater nostalgia
than a day in the blueberry woods:
berry-blue skies, a warming sun,
the clatter of crows, the chatter of kin,
and tow-headed children with blueberry grins.

A One-Year-Old Learns About Motion

Some things move by themselves
The robin cocking its head on the deck railing
The maple tossing its branches in the wind

Some things he can move himself
The bits of cracker he tosses from high chair to carpet
The cup he sends spinning across the tabletop

Some things refuse to move although he calls and gestures
The stack of paper he wants to crumple
The water glass on the counter beyond his reach

And the faces in the photographs
That stare at him and never change
No matter how often he smiles

The Barn in the Blizzard

Fitful blasts drive icy snow
nudging the timber-frame beams
'til mortise and tenon groan
and the linking oak pins creak.
Gusts swirl in the cupola
where whirling wind-devils yowl
like cats mating in the mow.

Frigid drafts of blizzard air
sneak beneath the sliding door
to sculpt furtive white fingers
reaching in across the floor.
Frigid strands of spider webs
hang like nets of frosty yarn,
spanning paisley-iced windows.

Cattle breathe in steamy heaves
with ears held back . . . uneasy.
The odor mix of mildewed hay,
rank manure, and sour silage
evokes a reflexive retch.
A fresh bale of straw is spread
to mitigate the foul stench.

Lights flicker, shadows flutter,
cows are anxious to be milked
by familiar herdsman's hands.
Wool cap buried in soft flanks,
he tugs milk from taut udders
in a steady spurt, spurt, beat
while the cold barn walls shudder.

The barn hunkers in the storm,
shivering like a critter
chilled to its extremities
fighting hypothermia,
while at its heart the herd is
gorging, fouling, and pulsing . . .
contented, secure and warm.

Man of the Year

This morning, the countryside had an orderliness about it, like a farm photograph on a feed store calendar. Hayfields are manicured green rectangles. Graded gravel roads run true north and south. Farmsteads—L-shaped white houses, hip-roofed red barns, green-treed yards, are neat and trim and precise.

This morning, Holsteins file lazily out of the dairy barn, drink from the stock tank, and wait near the gated lane to be driven to pasture. Pigs root in the shade of the pen; others lie on their sides in mud, warming to the sun. Sheep graze unconcerned, unfenced in the tall grass of an abandoned orchard.

This morning, the sun urges moss roses open in vivid pinks and yellows and oranges in the rock garden. Chickens scratch and peck in the dusty driveway. A retired Chesapeake Retriever sleeps on the granary stoop. Indifferent cats groom themselves in the aroma of fresh cut hay stacked on the wagon. A Mourning Dove coos a baleful cry.

Young Mick plays in the yard while his father Mel Fritz finishes chores in the barn. Mother Elaine referees the school-age kids in the house, reciting her litany of morning instructions. *Eat some toast. Keep your eyes on the clock. Don't forget your lunch money.*

The kids zip from room to room, gathering homework off the piano, yelling for help to find a missing shoe, watching out the kitchen window for the bus. Across the kitchen on a picture wall, framed photographs document early lives of these children: baptisms, first days of school, visits to Santa; and the early lives of their parents: Elaine's nursing school graduation portrait, Mel's picture in U.S. Army uniform, mounted and framed beside a cover of *TIME* magazine.

The school bus rounds the corner of the road, and the screen door swings open as kids sprint down the worn ruts of the driveway. Mick watches them board the bus and traces a road with a stick in the dirt to the granary. A mother hen cluck-clucks her newly hatched brood to the rotting remains of a haystack. The chicks mimic mother hen, stray from the flock, and are clucked back. Mick watches the yellow babies wander and return, scratch and peck. Mother hen pecks her way to the hay wagon. The cats, groomed and stoic, eye the chicks. An old tom jumps from the wagon and crouches by a tire.

Mick runs for the cat, picks it up, and carries it to the stock tank. The cat hisses and claws at Mick, scratches his arms and face, and jumps to the ground. Mick screams, extends his bleeding arms, as if waving to the school bus as it leaves the driveway. The mother hen squawks and screeches, calling the chicks. A rooster joins the melee.

Mel runs from the barn, freezes when he sees the bleeding child, hears his screaming and the screeching chickens. He freezes. Blood. Screams. What starts as a slow, high-pitched whistle in his head grows shrill, sharp, deafening. The ground vibrates. The granary rumbles and rocks. Dust rises from the ground and falls from the building. Through the dust comes the smell of smoke. Mel runs blindly for the boy and clutches him.

That November morning in 1967, two months before the Tet Offensive, breakfast for Charlie and Delta Squads was the usual—powdered eggs in an C-ration cup, warmed over a C-4 explosive. Sergeant Mel Fritz milled with somber infantrymen around the quiet camp, eating, drinking coffee, smoking. The air was heavy with an impenetrable menace, like any day before patrol. A flock of babbler birds screeched a threat high in the canopy of kapok trees. Monkeys bouncing around the periphery of the camp screamed and chattered. Delta Squad was hosting the visit of David Duncan, *TIME-LIFE* photographer. Mr. Duncan was a celebrity, a source of battle anecdotes and ties to New York. He was also a man of courage, shooting only his Leica, with an unused sidearm for protection.

That November morning, Charlie Squad patrolled the bombed-out Placu region of Vietnam where Allies and Vietcong had see-sawed control. They approached a rural village which was a moonscape of charred wall studs surrounding smoldering ash heaps. Abandoned carts and discarded furniture littered the roadways. A surviving pig scrambled from a pile of rotting garbage at the sight of the advancing infantry.

The Vietcong had fortified themselves well and won support of the few remaining inhabitants. The American presence was threatening, intimidating. Children cowered in front of the GIs, twice as big as their fathers, who transported an array of hardware from another galaxy. The pressure was on both sides to secure the area around Placu before the monsoons.

That November morning, Charlie Squad reconnoitered a nearly deserted village near Encau as a base for an offensive into the mountains to the north. One mountain was the site of a suspected military base, complete with strategic and tactical headquarters, ammunition depot, and military hospital. Charlie Squad had made recon missions through the town, working to gain trust of the few remaining inhabitants, old disabled people and a few children. In time, the children warmed to the GIs and worked their generosity, following them up the pocked trail north of town.

"C-rations? Cigarettes? Gum?" they called.

That November morning, Mel stopped to take a radio message from battalion headquarters. "A Vietcong formation is moving down the trail toward your village. Take cover. Do not engage. Then return to base." The message repeated for Delta Squad, also in the area.

The squad scattered in groups of three, Mel's trio finding refuge behind a demolished adobe and pole structure, the remains of a barn. Once settled, they listened for the squawk of jungle birds—parrots, babblers, and parakeets. In the quiet of the village, a rooster crowed, cooking utensils clinked in a makeshift hut, children giggled in an open square. Mel calculated from the birds screeching that he had time to coax the children to safety. A burned bus lay overturned along the road, tires scorched, paint bubbled and peeling, windows shattered. He ran toward the children, motioning for them to follow him and, scooping the smallest one in his arm, he headed for the bus. The children thought it was a game and followed him. He dumped a pocket of C-rations inside the bus and motioned for the children to stay down.

They scampered for the C-rations, and Mel ran for cover, safely out of distance but in view of the bus. The Vietcong formation was closer now, not visible but within hearing range—the clank of weapons against canteens, the scuffle of boots, whistles that mimicked the bird calls. The soldiers reached the northern edge of the village, creating a cloud of dust as they trampled the ruts and pot holes. The platoon leader signaled a halt and the platoon stopped. The elders of the village retreated to their huts; the children remained hidden in the bus. The pig snorted from the trash pile.

A rifle shot. Two Vietcong soldiers ran to the struggling pig, slit its throat with a bayonet, and carried it by the legs, spasmodic and bleeding, to the platoon leader.

The rifle shot and the shrill squeals of the pig aroused the children. One by one, they stood to look out the empty windows at the formation. Two soldiers approached the bus. While one watched the children, rifle ready, the other crawled inside. He backed out, followed by his rifle. On the bayonet was a C-ration bag in an olive drab wrapper with a U.S. stencil. He carried it to the platoon leader who shouted an order and motioned for the formation to proceed. Two Vietcong soldiers stood by as the others passed through town. When the formation was clear of the bus, one soldier jerked a grenade from his belt, pulled the pin, and made an easy lob high in the air. The soldiers ran toward the formation.

The grenade arced high and descended dreamily, striking the side of the bus, rolling along the window ledge. No sound. No sight of the children. The Vietcong rounded the bend in a trail of red dust.

A sudden explosion. Dust. Smoke. Steel splintered and rocketed. Sheet metal, torn ragged, soared in jagged chunks. The dust settled, replaced by clouds of acrid black smoke. Leaves floated down in erratic confusion, like charred confetti.

Mel ran into the smoke, blinded, not breathing. The smoke thickened as he neared the burning skeleton of the bus. He pulled goggles from his field pack, jerked his helmet aside, and slipped the goggles over his head. The structure of the bus was visible now. Through the smoke, he saw remains of upholstered seat cushions smoldering, silhouetted against a hole torn into the side of the bus. He saw movement under the dashboard in front of the driver's seat—a small child, the one he carried into the bus, crouched in a fetal fold.

The exploding grenade echoed up the valley and aroused the concern of recon's Delta Squad who arrived at the village as Mel ran from the burning bus, carrying the small blackened child out of the smoke. Sergeant Mel, looking otherworldly in his goggles, helmet askew, and a handkerchief tied over his nose and mouth, ran with the child. Photographer Duncan's lens caught the image of terror in the screaming child, the extended arms, the bleeding face.

Mr. Duncan requested that Mel sign a release that night, and he did. The photo made *TIME*'s cover when the American GI was designated 1968 Man of the Year.

After the parades, the parties, the reunions; after the newspaper stories, the Sergeant Mel Fritz Commemorative Day; after the nightmares, the out-on-your-ass drinking sprees, the taming of reflexes; after the wasted separation pay check; after the phone stopped ringing; after the world went back to work, Mel returned to the farm. He married Elaine, and now they have the four kids. His daily routine is predictable—morning chores, field work, evening chores; his seasonal rhythm is gratifying—plow and plant, cultivate and harvest.

This morning, he sits on the ground, leaning against a gnarly box elder tree, exhausted, shivering, and sweat-soaked. He dampens his tremors with a confused child hugged in his arms. Some days, his world holds together. Some days, it doesn't.

Three Men's Hands

I.
Chapped by ice-choked water,
scarred hands haul fish nets
from a grudging sea.
Sausage-size fingers spoke outward,
meaty palms ply wooden oars,
pull buoy lines, anchor ropes.

He sits upon a rocky shore;
gossamer threads held by clubbed fingers
weave spidery fishing webs.

II.
Scabbed fingers hold tools
in a power-clenched grip,
broken, dirt-lined nails
worn back to living flesh.
Grease-anointed hands
reef lug nuts free.

He stands at his bench;
fine-threaded bolts in gnarly fingers
turn smoothly into place.

III.
Twisted and broken from toil,
swollen hands heft bricks and blocks,
smear mud between flat faces,
set stone to mend a broken wall.
Hardened in lime-soaked sands,
callused hands chisel chunks of granite.

He stoops and gently scoops
his baby girl from off the floor,
tenderly wipes away her tear.

The Artist Within

The image holds me and won't let me go.
How did the artist know
to use the color that seeps into my veins
and flows through me like blood?
The painting whispers to me,
"I know you. I've been there too."
I want to be the artist who creates
with such boldness;
unspoken truths suggested
with a simple curving line.

Inspired, I prepare to paint,
but hold back. Fear of being ordinary
seizes my spirit and renders the artist within me
inarticulate. I pull myself together with
tenacity and conviction,
then fill my brush with pigment.
I pause, suspending the moment.
My intention overcomes my hesitation
as I touch the paintbrush
to the empty white canvas.

Summer Anthem

Cicadas drone in the heavy heat of day,
strident songs piercing August air clogged
with the scent of freshly mowed grass.
Charmeuse wings swish through dappled
pleats of reignited sunshine, scatter sunbeams
like shelled peas on a kitchen floor.
Shadows gather where the past and
future collide. Muddled delirium hovers.

The Beach Club, 1971

A teenage girl in a bikini lay on her stomach, arguing with her boyfriend over a plastic daisy. She kept planting it in the sand and he kept yanking it out.

"You leave my flower alone! I'm mad at you." I couldn't hear his response but I heard her giggles. "You're a naughty, naughty boy."

I sat on a towel behind them, gloomily fascinated by their banter. I knew this girl had to be popular. At the age of twelve, I also knew that as much as I wanted to be popular in high school, I could never talk in a baby voice or fight over a plastic daisy. What I enjoyed at the Beach Club was playing on the water top, sliding down the big curved slide, and racing with Julie Bauerdorff to the raft—not the adult one, but the raft off the middle beach that kids goofed around on despite warnings from the life guard.

The Beach Club was really a water-filled quarry with truckloads of sand brought in to make it look like a beach. My mother had come here when she was a teenager. Michigan Beach, people called it then, after Chicago's Lake Michigan. I loved hearing my mother's stories about an older Joliet. She and her three sisters had lived in a house on McDonough, not far from the canal. Back then, the canal hadn't separated West Side white neighborhoods from East Side black neighborhoods as it did today. Back then, my mother said, the block she grew up on was a mix of black and white families doing their best to get by. Mom's best friend was a little black girl named Ellen.

Hugging my knees on my hot pink and orange towel, I could see I-80's twin steel bridges arcing above the Des Plaines river in the distance. The other side of the lake was fringed with trees whose green branches sank heavily into water. I wondered what lay beyond those trees. How did you get there? You could walk only so far along the water until a chain-linked fence barred your path.

Julie Bauerdorff, who lived two houses down from me until she moved away in fourth grade, would definitely not be interested in whatever was behind those trees. Julie tanned better than me and her long blond hair was

149

straighter. She wasn't popular yet but I guessed it was only a matter of time before she moved into the cool group at her school.

I knew I should stand up to Julie more. When we were little, we played with another neighborhood girl, Dayle, who was two years younger than us. Sometimes Julie coaxed me to sneak away and leave plump little Dayle by herself. I was too much of a coward to say *No, that's mean, I won't.* I was still a coward. Earlier today, Julie said how glad she was there were no *niggers* at the Beach Club.

"You shouldn't say that word," I murmured, feeling my face redden.

"Why not, my dad lets me say it. He says the goop they wear in their hair would make the water greasy. He's right."

Instead of challenging Julie, I changed the subject. *Gutless wonder!* I liked Angie, the one black student in our seventh grade class. Angie had transferred to St. Patrick's three years ago. Before she joined our class, nuns talked gravely to us about the need for brotherly love and tolerance. It was embarrassing. I wondered if Angie saw through the fake friendliness of some of the popular kids, the ones who called her Ang*eline* and laughed really loud at her jokes.

It was during Angie's first year at St. Pat's that Martin Luther King, Jr. was killed and there was rioting on the East Side. Newspeople called King a great leader but our fourth grade teacher, Mrs. Hamer, considered him a rabble-rouser. *If this man is for peace,* she asked us, *then why does violence always follow him?*

That was the way my dad thought, too, although he never said *nigger* the way Julie Bauerdorff's father did. Mr. Bauerdorff and my dad worked together at Uniroyal when I was younger. My father didn't like Jim Bauerdorff. I didn't like him either. He wore his dark hair slicked back and stuck a pack of cigarettes under the sleeve of his T-shirt like a tough guy. He used a belt on Julie's two brothers.

I lay back on the towel. The beach was crowded today, but only with white families. This would have struck anyone who wasn't from Joliet as odd since The Beach Club was on the East Side of town, in the middle of a black neighborhood. It was rumored that the owner screened applications and automatically rejected any from blacks. Did my parents know this? It was wrong to be prejudiced, but I secretly didn't mind that the Beach Club admitted only whites. Some of the black kids at Inwood Swimming Pool scared me. They were loud and mean and broke into lockers. I could not imagine ever being best friends with a black girl.

"Earth to Tolf. Earth to Tolf." Julie plopped down next to me, slurping a root beer popsicle. "You look a million miles away. What're you thinking about?"

"Nothing. Just lying here."

"Let's get back in the water after I'm done eating this."

"Okay."

Sun glinted on the tiny gold crucifix Julie wore on a delicate chain around her neck. She didn't wear it for decoration, she told me; she wore it to remind herself that she was a Christian and a Catholic. It was a perfect day to swim, windless and very hot. Julie and I tore off our T-shirts and ran toward cool water.

Late, Sunday Afternoon

Resting is Saturday's desperate need.
On the dirty hem of a week wrestled
like every one before it, I put off laundry,
loose bolts, gritty floor tiles, stinky toilets,
shaggy hedges, lost buttons, weeds.
Bills look to Monday for payment.

Now, Sunday, holy day of rest,
by my own inaction rife with bitter fruit.
At this late hour we negotiate—
Body pines for respite and ease,
Conscience frets chores underdone,
Frenetic week ahead, obstinate,
refuses any hope I had at all
of absolution.

Dear Rosalie

Remember, before you moved, we rushed weekly around
    the crowded gym.
Our tennis shoes beat the inside track. Eyes on the clock,
    we breakneck talked.

Visiting you now, an entire day opens up. California
    mountains surround us.
Bony clouds, streaked and pinked, brush sage, dust rock,
    sweep redwood and pine.

Suddenly a hawk dangles from the sky. Its red tail dips and
    circles a bird we can't identify.
Crow? Magpie? Side by side, they ride airwaves, and coast,
    and rise.

You and I ascend with them, shear blue-gray skies, glide
    live with the bird planes.
Toes tucked in, skirts flapping, women nearing sixty,
    winging our way home.

Language

Tired of the political bickering and name calling in every
    media form
Bored by the inane chatter in the grocery line
Annoyed at the profanity lacing the passing conversations
    on the street

I unfold my lawn chair on the back deck and lean back
To watch the constellations navigating their way slowly
    across the night
Where they eddy through the silence in ancient lyrical
    eloquence

Foosha

"Daddy! Daddy! Lookit the green one! Lookit the yellow one!" The hood on the girl's coat fell over her eyes and she pushed it back with one hand and pointed at the cars with the other. "Daddy! I like the red one! Let's get the red one!"

Overhead, little plastic triangles showed the movements of a flickering winter wind. The flags made cold snapping sounds and the cars in the rows stood at attention for the little girl to review. She ran ahead and found a patch of ice and skidded across on rubber-soled boots. She met the pavement on the other side and fell, mittened hands outstretched. Her father circled the skim of ice and picked her up. She cried briefly and resumed her litany of colors in his arms.

They walked in front of the grills of the cars, the girl announcing the primary colors. She had learned the names of the colors from a box of crayons he had given her for her birthday. When they came upon a car of a color she didn't know, she paused. She took off her mittens and they dangled from the clip on a cord inside her coat. She held up her fingers and said, "Not red, not blue, not green," and each time she announced a color she held down a finger. When she ran out of fingers, she turned to her father and asked, "What color is that?"

He answered her, holding her in his arms, saying, "Well, honey, I'd call it fuchsia."

She laughed, saying over and over, "Foosha, foosha." Now, any car that she didn't know the color of became "foosha."

He put her down, remarking to himself that it wasn't so long ago he could have carried her for hours and never noticed the weight. She didn't run ahead now but stayed near his side saying softly, "Foosha, foosha."

Squeezing through the cars, coming from the direction of the little tin cabin on the lot, was a large man in a spring jacket with his hands tucked under his armpits. He smiled as he caught the eye of the girl's father and grunted as he made his way between two Fords.

"Hello there, little girl! Just get your driver's license?" He laughed, and the men shook hands. The salesman's hands went back under his armpits.

"The name's Joe Olson, and if there's anything I can show you, well, you just go ahead and ask. I see she likes our 'foosha' model! Aren't women something? They can be on the lot for just a few minutes, and right away they pick out the best car!" He chuckled and asked, "Can I get you some coffee? Or maybe a little hot chocolate?" He winked at the little girl and her eyes widened. She stopped saying "foosha" and said, "Daddy! Can I have some hot chockie?"

Her father rubbed his hands together and said, "It is getting kind of frosty out here. You think that some hot chocolate would help us make a decision?"

The little girl clapped her hands together and cried, "Hot chockie, Daddy! Hot chockie!"

Her father smiled at her and looked at the salesman and said, "Well, I'll bet that would taste good, but right now I'd like to know how much this here 'foosha' car is."

The salesman laughed and said, "What'd I say, what'd I say? The little lady can pick 'em, can't she? Well sir, this here is a four-door, six-cylinder $3,500 'foosha'!"

The father looked down at his daughter and asked, "Is this the one you want, honey? Are you sure you don't want the red one, or the green one, or the yellow one?"

She grabbed the bottom of her father's coat and said in a mock grimace, "No, Daddy. I told you and I told you. I want the 'foosha' and I want hot chockie!"

The father lifted her up in his arms and turned to the salesman. "Well, when her mind is made up, it stays made up. We'll take the 'foosha' and a little of that coffee you offered."

On the way to the salesman's shack, the little girl asked to be put down. She ran ahead between the parked cars. When they reached the door of the shack, the salesman pulled the door open and the little girl and her father walked in. The little girl turned and curtsied. The salesman took a small pot that sat steaming on a hot plate and poured out a cupful of hot chocolate for the little girl. On another hot plate was a pot of coffee. He took a cup and filled it for the father. As he passed the coffee he said,

"Yessir, that sure is one sweet little girl you've got there. Been married long?"

"Long enough not to ask stupid questions. Give me the keys to the car." With a quick movement, the father pulled a nickel-plated revolver from the waistband of his slacks.

"Now get down on the floor, Joe, and don't move for ten minutes." The little girl held up her arms to be picked up and she settled onto her father's shoulder. Keeping his gun on the salesman, he reached into his daughter's coat pocket and pulled out a stack of money with the bank wrapper still around it. He snapped the wrapper and peeled off two fresh bills. "Here's a little friendly advice." He stuffed the bills into the salesman's clenched hand.

"C'mon honey, let's go for a ride in our new 'foosha.' And be careful with that hot chocolate."

Miz Sharkey, My Haven

A haven for a small girl was she,
and that small fatherless girl, me.
My mother widowed by malaria,
a beautiful woman of thirty,
in the dark days of the Great Depression,
so burdened, trying to eke out
a living for her brood of four.
She had no inkling of the terrors I felt
from the ignorant men and boys who found me
an innocent prey to their advances.
Miz Sharkey may have sensed my pain
and confusion over what happened
again and again, but she never spoke of it.
She sat in her rocking chair
in her voile dress with the blue flowers
and butterflies, soft voice, gentle demeanor,
fed me cookies and milk, gave me a dress of her
          daughter's,
Louise Dudley Sharkey, all grown up and moved away.
She gave me books, *The Girl of The Limberlost* and
          Pollyanna.
I read and re-read them, especially *Pollyanna*.
Thus, Miz Sharkey gave me tools
to deal with the pain and vulnerability:
"There's something in every experience to be glad about."
She asked Mother to let her adopt me.
I have often wished that might have been.

The Pearl

The ugly helmet
protected his head
and they stared.
His awkward hand
missed the crucial catch
and they yelled.
His lone hand rose
to agree with the teacher
and they laughed.

He wanted to be like them.
He cried and we cried with him.
He endured the pain of his
uniqueness and like the pearl
was rubbed beautiful.

Poetry - LuAnne L White
Just Before the River Freezes

A shadow V shimmers on steel grey
reflection from the sky
the water heavy not breaking, foaming, bubbling but
rolling long behind green-headed mallards.
Snow floats from nowhere
to land on their heads and feathers.
Bottoms up—
stopping for lunch.

Belle Fourche Harry

The Belle Fourche River cuts a wide deep valley, winding through western South Dakota's rolling prairie. This isolated ranching country is straight out of the Old West with far flung villages named Hereford, White Owl, and Elm Springs. It's also some of the best mule deer hunting territory east of Wyoming. My father and I felt lucky to have drawn non-resident deer licenses for this area. But that was only half the battle. As lowly tourist hunters from Minnesota, we needed to find a hunting spot in this area of strictly private land where hunting privileges are usually reserved for friends, relatives, or high paying clients. So Dad, the fearless farmer-turned-insurance-agent, started knocking on ranch house doors, and kept knocking until he found Harry.

Harry looked like he belonged there. He was in his mid-sixties and as stout, weathered gray, and tough as the gnarled cottonwood trees lining the banks of the river. He welcomed us, helped set up our camper on a deserted farm site, and gave us the run of several thousand acres of prime deer country.

We soon found out Harry was aptly named. It was early November and the prairie winds were cold even for us natives of frigid Minnesota. Harry would show up every morning to milk the lone cow that mingled with the beef cattle in the corral. He milked the cow by hand from a stool, dressed in only jeans and a flannel shirt while we stood by bundled in our warmest hunting clothes. The plaid flannel shirt was always unbuttoned halfway down, with ample gray chest hair sprouting profusely from it like the hide of a winter-toughened animal.

There were other things about Harry that fit the tough old rancher stereotype. Like his absolute hatred of coyotes. I watched one repeatedly tilt its head back and howl at the sunrise the first morning. I held my fire, content to observe this primeval scene and not disturb any nearby deer. When Harry rumbled up in his old Ford pickup later in the morning, I made the mistake of telling him. He launched into an expletive-laced, anti-varmint tirade that lasted several minutes. It ended with an ultimatum. He leaned out of his pickup window, finger pointing directly at me, and made things perfectly clear. "If you are going to hunt on my property, you will shoot and kill—or at least wound—every damn coyote you see!"

Okay, when in Rome . . .

I managed to shoot the next coyote I saw and got another lesson in life on the Dakota prairie. An elderly woman lived in an old homestead above the ravine where I was hunting. She walked down the fence line to meet me and called out down the hill, "I heard shots. Did you get your deer?"

"Nope," I yelled back. "Just a toothless old coyote." I lugged the scarred old male up the hill and instantly made a new friend.

"Thank you, thank you!" She literally danced with excitement, hopping from foot to foot on what had to be eighty-year-old legs, and finally actually hugging me. "That one's been eating my chickens every night! I can sleep again!"

I guess it's pretty hard to enjoy the lonesome howl of a coyote when you are worrying about the livestock that provides your livelihood and the food on your table.

We soon learned that the more time you spent with Harry, the more you learned about the dangers of stereotypes and assumptions. He stopped by our campsite every evening, obviously hungry for company and conversation. We heard plenty of stories about hard prairie life and his younger days in rough-and-tumble cow towns. But we also heard about his wife and family. He married late in life to an older woman with what many men would consider too much baggage. A birth defect had left her with only one hand and she had a son from a previous marriage. The son had died ten years before, under suspicious circumstances, in the dark alley of a city hundreds of miles away. Harry still mourned and wondered why.

And hang out with Harry and his wife and you soon learned a new definition of self-sufficiency. While neighboring ranchers were poisoning the grasshoppers plaguing their wheat fields, he cultivated habitat for sharp-tailed grouse and gray partridge. These grasshopper-eating game birds were so numerous they got in the way—flushing loudly from thickets in the ravines of the river valley, spooking the deer we were quietly trying to stalk.

Lunch at his spacious but simple ranch house was home-canned venison, cooked in thick gravy and poured over potatoes and vegetables from the garden. The milk came from that cow at our campsite and the fresh baked bread was made from wheat he grew and personally ground to flour. *The Mother Earth News* would have loved to interview Harry and his wife. However, I'm not sure Harry would have been flattered.

We never did get a deer on that trip some twenty-five years ago. We did spend a long week roaming the hills, collecting memories, and hanging out with Harry. Those memories somehow seem more important than any deer. I know Harry is long since gone and not around to welcome me back to his ranch. But I might head back to the Belle Fourche River country sometime soon anyway. I know times have changed. But I'm really hoping where there was one Harry, there are more.

Heartwood

It takes trust and practice, tangential splits
over and under, we become woven and wrapped
with curlicue overlays, we chase and stitch;
with fingers, entwined, sticky with sap,
we have learned to glide, over grain lines;
row by row, we split, we splice, we turn-back.
We are no boring braid—no fillers of time,
our pieces seasoned, yet never brash.
For we have broken the hickory wedge;
just to make a handle, we dove into the pith,
the heartwood—where many lovers fear to dredge.
For you have mended ten years of pain with your lips,
held my head in your lap while I unraveled for miles.
Come, taste my love in this kiss. Let me carry you awhile.

Without You

I long for you
the way a December body
yearns for April.

In the cellar of myself
I store you in summer's syrup,
tuck you into my soft root bin.

Your voice, your laughter
blown away by a shrill wind.
I am an abyss without an echo.

I have something to tell you
but I cannot speak
with lips unkissed.

More Than Surgery

He avoids surgery
until the pain
is unbearable—
my big strong husband,
always in control.

So when I see him
in his hospital gown and cap,
an I.V. trailing from his arm,
resignation and surrender in his eyes,
it takes me by surprise.

My forced smiles and
rambling small talk
fill the nervous space between us
until he is wheeled
into the operating room.

I pray and pace
and wait and worry
and wander through the gift shop,
feigning interest in cards and flowers
and fuzzy slippers,

trying not to imagine
him lying there helpless,
trying not to picture
what they are doing
to my big strong husband.

In these moments,
when life is altered
from a wispy white cloud
into a gray thunderhead
and the rain releases in torrents,

we huddle for warmth,
emerging either drenched
or damp
or dry
but together.

The Ultrasound

Anna and her husband sat in the third floor waiting room of the Charlton Building. It was early morning and Obstetrics wasn't busy. A handful of pregnant women rested magazines on their ample bellies.

Anna hadn't finished the stack of paperwork when her buzzer went off. She and Miles got to their feet.

A long-faced nurse reached for the buzzer. "Name?"

"Anna Lorenzo."

"Date of birth?"

"Seven fourteen seventy-six."

"Your first appointment is with the Genetic Counselor."

A young doctor with shoulder-length red hair stood to greet them. "I'm Dr. Lackey."

They shook hands.

"I assume you're here because of your age," the doctor said, consulting paperwork. "You're thirty-five, which isn't old, of course. But that's the age data shows an increase in serious birth defects."

"That's what I had read," Anna replied.

Dr. Lackey laid a chart before them. "When a woman has a Level II Ultrasound, we discuss the possible findings prior to the test. Generally the results aren't conclusive, but we look for indicators that would *increase* your chances of having a baby with a genetic abnormality— either with the sex chromosomes, in which case the baby probably wouldn't survive the pregnancy, or with an extra twenty-one chromosome, which indicates Down's Syndrome."

Miles took Anna's hand.

Pointing to the chart, the doctor said. "At your age, the baby's probability of a chromosomal abnormality is very minimal."

Yes, Anna thought, *one in three hundred isn't terrible odds, unless you're that unlucky "one."*

"How far along are you?"

"Twenty weeks."

Dr. Lackey frowned. "That doesn't give you a lot of time if something is wrong, which we don't anticipate. In Minnesota, a pregnancy can be terminated up until the twenty-first week. If the results might lead you to consider that option, you would need to decide quickly."

Anna felt as if the air had gone out of the room.

"The ultrasound takes close to an hour. Have you had an ultrasound before?"

Anna nodded. "With my first pregnancy. We have a four-year old."

"The Level II is the same, only the technician will look at those indicators or markers that would increase your baby's risk factor." Dr. Lackey folded her hands on her desk. "Questions?"

Miles spoke. "Will we have the results today?"

"Yes, the technician will take the necessary measurements and pictures, and those will be sent to the Perinatologist, Dr. Walker, for review. You'll meet with him after the ultrasound."

Dr. Lackey handed Anna her card and smiled reassuringly. "This can be a lot of information to take in. If you have questions later, don't hesitate to call."

In the exam room, a dark-skinned woman pressed buttons on a small machine. "I'm Katie," the technician said, looking up from the sonogram equipment. "Go ahead and lie down. I'll get you gelled."

Anna lay on the padded table. She rolled her shirt up to her bra and pushed the stretchy band of her pregnancy pants down to her underwear.

"Don't worry," Katie smiled, as she held the gel bottle. "It's warm.

"I'll explain what we're looking at as we go. We'll start with baby's head—specifically the skin at the neck fold, then the brain and the top of the spinal column. We'll also look at the internal organs, including the heart and its chambers. I'll measure bone length in the arms, legs, and hands. After that, Dr. Walker will explain the results."

Katie moved the transducer wand over Anna's stomach, watching the screen as she spoke. "Will you be finding out baby's sex today?"

"Yes."

"You don't want it to be a surprise?"

"I'm not much for surprises."

Gray, black and white images swam across the small screen as Katie moved the transducer with her right hand and clicked the keyboard with her left. Anna and Miles watched intently, but it was hard to know what they were looking at.

A half-hour in, Katie said, "Everything is looking good. Let's see if we can tell if baby is a girl or a boy.

"Okay, we're in the right place. Yes, here's baby's bottom and here's . . . ."

"Baby's penis," said Miles.

"Boy number two," smiled Anna.

"It's a boy," Katie looked pleased. She typed BOY on the screen next to baby's bottom and took a picture.

Anna lay back on the table.

"We're a little more than halfway, now."

"We'll have to discuss names over lunch," Miles said.

Anna nodded. "Maybe we could go to that restaurant-"

"Oh," Katie said sharply, and they looked at her. "Oh," she repeated, frowning. "Well, I'm seeing something unusual—"

"What is it?" Miles strained to get a better look.

"See baby's feet?"

The small white feet showed clearly on the screen.

"They're twisted," she demonstrated with her left hand. "He'll be born with club feet. I'm so sorry. It's the most common birth defect besides cleft palate."

Anna's heart thumped. "What does that mean?"

"Dr. Walker will explain in more detail. But basically baby will need casts to correct the position of his feet."

"Will he walk?" Miles asked loudly.

"Yes. In the past, he would have always walked awkwardly. But the treatment is so advanced that once the corrections are made in his first year, no one will be able to tell he ever had club feet."

"How did this happen?"

Katie shook her head. "It's nothing either of you did—nothing to do with your age or diet or anything. It just happens. We don't know why."

Anna and Miles waited in Dr. Walker's office.

"Well . . . ." Miles trailed off.

"She didn't see anything wrong neurologically. She said club feet doesn't indicate any other birth defects."

"After those statistics Dr. Lackey showed us," Miles said, "I almost feel like we're getting off easy."

Anna nodded, relieved.

"If something has to be wrong . . . ."

"This isn't so bad," Anna finished.

They sat for a moment in silence.

"So . . ."

"Yes?" Anna looked at Miles.

"We'd better start thinking of names."

First Apartment

I hummed as I folded the clean clothes I had carried up to our third floor, share-a-bath-with-the-couple-across-the-hall apartment. My gaze drifted around the room. I knew just the spot for a small Christmas tree. The sofa my grandmother gave us sagged, but it held good memories. I liked the color. The table had one short leg. The tilt added a little drama to meals, and somehow we never got around to leveling it. One burner on the small stove refused to heat, but I couldn't cook much, anyway. A frame of 2x4s with a sheet tacked across the front served as a closet. Our clothes did not fill it. The mattress rolled both of us to the middle. We liked it that way. Sure, money was tight. Jim was a third year college student with a part-time job; I was a secretary. Wait, they said. We didn't. I loved folding Jim's clothes. It was somehow so . . . intimate. The door burst open and there he was, tall, strong, and reaching for me. The sun shone in the uncurtained windows and his blue eyes turned bluer. He grabbed me and swung me around. Our first home spun into a splendid blur.

Down Under My Heart

I adopt Australia
as my other country.
Not in a formal ceremony,
but as an adoption of love,
a connection with the spirit of
the land and the people.
The energy of the ages which inhabits Uluru,
the twisted trees and powdered sugar shores
that meet the aqua sea at Whitehaven Beach
will always be part of me.
Back in Minnesota I go about my life,
singing "Waltzing Matilda" under my breath,
closing my eyes to see
the Southern Cross in the night sky,
and caring about the survival of the
endangered cassowary bird.
I imagine meeting the Aboriginal artist who
made the earth-red bracelet I wear with affection.
I will cheer on the Aussies at the Olympics.
I wonder how droughts or floods or cyclones
affect my friends in Port Macquarie and Melbourne.
I will forever carry within me
the essence of the rain forest and coral reef
and the life force of the outback.

A Fateful Day

Wednesday afternoon had been long. She thought the company board would readily accept her budget proposal; after four hours of intense debate, they did. Seldom did she lose. She was tired and was looking forward to relaxing in her suite.

Grace rarely regretted her decisions. Decisions calculated to fit her life. However, she was perplexed about her feelings for Brett. Feelings she had never expected. She'd given him an ultimatum: either he accepted or never advance in the company. Today she would have his answer.

When Hugo Turner, president of Oxford Manufacturing, interviewed Grace Agile, he was impressed. She was quick and smart. He never regretted hiring her.

"Grace, I know you're aware of problems at our Omaha office. In your five years here, you've proved to be very capable. I want you to take over the manager's position in Omaha. You'll fly back to Newark for executive meetings, and a promotion when you return."

Two years later, Turner welcomed Grace into his office.

"You've been looking forward to this day and, as promised, a promotion to second vice president. Would you consider it?"

She was aware the position was open and readily accepted the offer.

"I'll walk you to your office." Hugo knew she was impressed, aware she wouldn't show it.

"Before you leave, stop in my office," he said closing the door.

Thirty-nine, second vice president of this prestigious company! She had planned her future, and it didn't include marriage or affairs. Her parents were killed in an accident when she was twenty-three, and no close relatives. She was beholden only to herself, her goal—to be highly successful.

"Grace, your position requires an assistant," Hugo said when she stopped at his office. "Hire someone, preferably within the company."

She knew exactly whom she wanted. Brett Morrison, her assistant in Omaha.

Brett Morrison was hired by Grayson Tool Company in Omaha the year he graduated from the University of Nebraska. Within three years, Brett became the assistant to the president. The same year he and Sylvia married.

Grace had been in Omaha for a year when Hugo asked her to be one of the presenters at the company's semi-yearly conference in Newark. The conference would be in the Victoria Plaza where Grace kept a private suite, one with expensive and comfortable furnishings. Her favorite purchase was a pastel picture called Morning Sunrise, the colors of the sky reflecting into a lake.

Grace invited representatives to the evening social hour in her suite, an opportunity to mingle with personnel who worked in regional and foreign offices. It was that evening she noticed Brett. She listened to his conversations, impressed with his business sense, self-assurance, and friendly disposition. She discovered he was from Omaha working for Grayson.

Six months after the conference, Grace's office manager left the company. She called Brett. Would he consider working with her in the Omaha office?

"Sylvia, I've been offered a job with Oxford Manufacturing Company. It sounds like a promising opportunity," Brett told Sylvia the day Grace's secretary called him.

"Is it here in Omaha?"

"Yes, I'd attend semi-yearly meetings in Newark, Oxford's headquarters."

"You know it would be hard for me to leave here."

Brett proved to be as competent as Grace thought, but there was something she had not foreseen—her physical attraction for him.

At the last conference in Newark, Grace asked Brett to stay after the social hour wanting to discuss the future of Oxford in Omaha.

Brett shouldn't have accepted the last drink. He knew his limit but it was comfortable sitting on the couch, and he was tired. Grace moved closer to him, placed her hand on his knee, and told him she was attracted to him.
When he awoke the next morning, Grace was gone. On the plane back to Omaha, he wrestled with his feelings. Would he tell Sylvia? What about his relationship in the Omaha office? Grace was discreet; only in Newark did the affair continue.

Brett took over Grace's position when she returned to Newark. He was at his desk when his secretary buzzed him to take a call from Ms. Agile.
"Good morning, Grace. How's the new vice president?"
"Brett, I need an assistant in my office. It is you I want and a great promotion. Call me back." The line clicked.
Brett sat upright. He would consider the promotion but thought of what Sylvia said when he told her he would be working for Oxford. *I wouldn't want to leave Omaha.*

Three days later, Brett's secretary buzzed him, "Call for you, Mr. Morrison."
"Brett, I haven't heard from you. Fly out and see what this promotion offers."
Brett flew to Newark and walked into Grace's well-appointed office. It was tempting to be at the headquarters.
"I can't tell Sylvia we are going to move. She loves Omaha and her family is there."
"Look Brett, I need you here. This is a great promotion for you. Bring Sylvia to Newark next week, and show her around. You can stay in my suite."
Grace could not let Brett go. There were times she questioned her feelings but dismissed any guilt about being involved with a married man, especially someone like Brett. She wanted him near her.
The offer was overpowering and, the more Brett thought about it, the more he wanted the position. He'd

like an office like Grace's. He made up his mind to accept. Now, to break the news to Sylvia.

"Sylvia," Brett said the evening he arrived from Newark, "on Monday we are going to Newark where we will stay at the Victoria Suites for two evenings, and Wednesday we will drive to the Poconos where we will rent a cabin."

"I have never been out east. Sounds great."

"I'll bring Sylvia out next Monday and leave on Wednesday morning," Brett phoned Grace after his conversation with Sylvia. Then Grace made a strange request.

"Do not call me from the suite. The only way I want to know if you take the offer is to hang the pastel painting by the door upside down; you know my favorite one. I want the answer the day you and Sylvia leave the suite.

"And Brett," she continued, "I will never offer you any opportunities to advance in this company if you don't agree to move to Newark."

Grace was sure he would accept.

The morning they left the suite, while Sylvia was showering, Brett quickly changed the painting. Only someone familiar would know it was hung upside down.

"I didn't mind waiting for you after I had driven the car out of the hotel garage, but I thought you were right behind me," Brett said when they stopped for lunch on the way up the mountains.

"Just was checking to see if I had left anything behind in the suite. And the strangest thing, on my way out I noticed the painting by the door was upside down, so I turned it around."

Living in Two Worlds

One is the here in our eyes,
Ears, nose, touch, that world
Of wondrous things.
Just pay attention:
It's enough to fall in love
With rivers, cars, cats,
Mountains, hibiscus,
Wine, and sweets for
Every sense.

And then there's the world
Beneath, where images swim
And words swarm.
It's no wonder sometimes
They detach, and we wander
In this space between:
Where are the car keys?
What's that word?
Where am I?

Skeleton

comes out of the closet,
clanks her way
to the sofa.
Make room,
watch her settle in,
crossing one leg bone over the other,
phalanges dangling,
couch pattern showing
through rib cage.

No conversation needed,
only this coming out.
Smile at her,
acknowledge that she is
not being dragged
behind the boat
or ruminating in storage.
Her familiar turn of ankle,
her drooping jaw,
are repeated
in your comfortable curves,
the warmth of your flesh.

No need to make small talk.
Smile.
Let her know
your pleasure in her presence.
Tell her to come again
or make up a bed for her
there on the couch.
Be glad she is not
the elephant in the room.

Margo Drives the Roadgrader

The city street repair crew had agreed to turn off their big machines during the funeral. This allowed the mourners to sit bathed in slanted October sun streaming golden through the stained-glass window. The sudden silence a metaphor for Margo's death after a life filled with drama and more recently filled with pain of COPD and emphysema.

She was a second wife—not the one who caused his divorce—and she had spent years attempting to win love and respect from his five grown children. In the early years, she planned events at their llama farm to delight the step-grandchildren; generally, their parents, after agreeing to come, failed to bring them. She remembered every birthday and holiday with cards for each of them. They ignored hers.

Margo had been a woman of savvy and importance as a fashion buyer for Dayton's Department Store in Minneapolis. She traveled to L.A. and New York to choose the styles that would sell to Minnesota women. Her artistic eye rarely made a mistake and she reveled in the business. Yet, after her own divorce, she had grown restless wanting more from life. That's when she met Jim in the barns at the State Fair. A strangely prophetic setting.

Jim, too, was dissatisfied with corporate hoop-jumping and dreamed of adventure and new love. Both had been reading the "back to the earth" books that were popular at the time. And, with the ultimate in daring, they cashed in their retirement funds and bought a barren farmstead and became llama breeders. Margo donned boots and flannel shirts. She dug out a watering hole, wormed and tended the animals. This city girl embraced the life-style with gusto. She never was a woman to do things halfway.

Their llama business was a success but, as they moved toward their sixties, their smoking habits began to impact their health. So they sold their animals and their farm and moved to a small college town with medical facilities. They bought a house overlooking the Mississippi River and delighted in the fox and rabbits and assorted birds that visited their backyard. Both Jim and Margo enrolled in classes and a new horizon opened to them. Margo embraced "Women's Studies" as though she had invented the course. Jim tried out for college theater and was cast in some plays. Life was good.

Until the day Jim collapsed in the bathroom with a double aneurysm and died several days later.

Once again, Margo reached out to the step-children. She arranged the funeral. Some of them came. The others would come some months later to his burial at Ft. Snelling Cemetery. Margo had to ride the bus down with Jim's urn in her lap.

Ironically, it was the first wife who was the kindest to her after the burial. The oldest son stashed her in a partially finished bedroom under the eaves. But he did agree to act as executor of his father's estate. Margo was relieved of at least that burden—only to have the son dump it back into her lap a few weeks later.

Margo began to focus more on the writing that she had started doing in college. She lived with assorted cats and dogs, all rescued from the local animal shelter. Poetry became her passion and she joined poetry groups, hosted groups of writers around her large dining room table (often with a cat walking across it as they talked). Her dream was to publish a book of her own poetry and that dream was realized the last year of her life.

Then, even though she had quit smoking, the effects necessitated her living connected to oxygen tanks. On her portable tank, she displayed a sign FORMER SMOKER. She confronted young women whom she saw smoking, asked them if they wanted to end up like her. She cared about others and always when eating out or shopping, observed name tags and spoke to those who waited on her. Only when some young manager treated her like an old woman who knew nothing about business, did her anger flare.

Now her battle is finished. Her friends gather to honor her and mourn her. She would have been surprised. She always thought no one would come to her funeral. She almost didn't have one until her lady pastor convinced her it was for the sake of her friends who needed a place to gather.

Her spirit may have been present because when that oldest step-son stood up to eulogize her, the silent earth-moving equipment roared back into operation, rattling pews and drowning out all the tributes he never gave her in life.

At Eighty

When the sun of our autumn days
begins to dim
the promise of winter brings
cold memories,
wrong steps
that can never be changed
bitter regrets that become immortal.

The hope of spring
comes from within.
Look for the birdsong of
love and friendship.
Find the warmth of the sun
in remembered laughter.
Let the light shine.

Forgive yourself again and again.
A life has been lived.
Halleluiah!

Flames on her Birthday
for Maxine Russell

When your friend turns one hundred
you think of the length of candles—
how you conserve, burn them less often,
to make the wax last a little longer.

When your friend turns one hundred
you feel spry as a sparrow
while you watch her navigate her walker,
or roll along in a creaky wheelchair.

When she reaches that age,
so ripe with reason, and golden,
she is out of your reach, so far
up a tree, she is seemingly out of sight.

You are the rooted one, tethered,
earthbound, while she breathes
charmed air, her borrowed time
better than any you've bought and paid for.

Mostly she sleeps through her tightrope life,
with one eye open for the final drum roll—
no longer a circus act of cooking and scrubbing,
juggled for years for family and friends.

No more menial tasks pushed her way.
Her way is to stay alive, just for today,
the accordion in and out of her lungs,
music to her half-deaf ears.

She knows the wick grows shorter,
the flame sputters; the candle lit now
for emergencies only, or special occasions,
like this one, her hundredth birthday.

Secrets of Gichigami

Twisted vines and foliage crouched closer as the gravel road wound back into the dense Minnesota forestland. Carrie slowed her speed, absorbed in thought, watching for her turn. She wanted desperately to leave Tony and move back to Nebraska, but how could she? Tony Stanton, son of the great Andrew J. Stanton, had sworn he'd never let her leave.

Tony's father, a prominent judge in Minneapolis, was a force to be reckoned with, a trait that had passed through the bloodlines. Could she trust the courts, knowing his father's realm of influence, even if it was 1980? Her girls were all that mattered to her. Mallory was eight, her little ballerina; Jessica, seven, a brown-eyed sweetie; and Anna, almost four, Mommy's girl.

Tony ran a road construction crew out of Minneapolis; they had met when he was assigned to a long stretch of I-80 west of Lincoln. Now a foreman, his crew was repairing the popular North Shore highway.

She'd left the girls with Tony's parents to drive up from Minneapolis to meet Tony for their anniversary. He'd instructed her to meet him at a restaurant the locals all raved about, tucked along the rocky bluffs of Lake Superior. She didn't feel like celebrating the past ten years as his wife, but decided the rendezvous might keep Tony from suspecting her intentions.

Carrie glanced at her hastily scribbled directions and turned into an opening under a looming canopy of tangled greenery. When the road narrowed to a rutty lane, she knew she was lost. She turned the wheel in a tight circle and felt the rear tire drop. Rocks *pinged* against the fender as she pressed the accelerator but the car didn't budge.

Tears burned her eyes. She was angry at herself for getting lost. Angrier at Tony for making her meet him at some backwoods supper club instead of the motel in town.

Carrie stepped from the car in her sandals and sundress, the warm, musky air clinging to her skin. A glint of sunlight reflecting on a mirror caught her eye. Two pickups were parked next to a rustic shack with a pitched roof and covered porch. Decades ago, it had been a general store, the boards weathered to a shiny black. Behind the store, a granite cliff jutted into the lake like a long finger, the blue-green waters swirling at the base in dizzying motion.

An uneasy feeling spread through Carrie's core. She hesitated, then heard voices echo over the water and eased her way past the shack. Two men, rough-looking sorts, were bent over another man, his head covered in blood. Was he injured?

She halted her steps as the men dragged the limp body toward the edge. It was then she noticed the concrete block tied to his waist. She watched in disbelief as they pushed him over the edge. Seconds later, she heard the splash.

Before she could turn to run, strong arms grabbed her from behind. Carrie kicked, trying to break free, but her efforts were useless. The man lifted her onto the porch, yelling at the other two. "Damn it, Sully!" he shouted, slamming the door behind them. "Make sure the coast is clear when we've got business to handle!" Scattered remnants of the former store were strewn about; crooked fixtures hung on the wall.

"Shane!" the other one yelled and tossed a rope.

A dank odor filled Carrie's nostrils as Shane thrust her into a chair. He pulled her arms back and tied the rope tight, cutting into her wrists. Carrie guessed he was in his thirties, not what she'd envisioned for a killer. He wore new jeans and a Bob Dylan T-shirt. In contrast, the other two were older and grittier, hicks to the bone.

"Well, well," Shane said, "somethin' tells me you're not a local. Where you from?" He had hawk-like features and his black hair touched his shoulders.

Carrie opened her mouth but no words came out. Her mind was numb, her breaths shallow.

"Talk to me." Shane pulled up a chair and leaned in close, his steel blue eyes penetrating. "What are you doin' out here all alone?"

"Meeting . . . my husband," she stammered.

"I'm afraid Sully here's put us in a bit of a predicament," he said, leaning back. "If I let you go, you'll run straight to the cops."

"No," Carrie said, shaking her head. "I won't tell a soul, *I promise.*" She met his steely eyes, pleading for understanding.

Shane folded his arms, studying her. "Eddie, get me a beer."

"Sure thing." Bottles clinked as Eddie opened an old brown refrigerator.

"*Please* . . . I have three little girls."

"See, this is an important pipeline for packages with great street value. No one hassles us at the border," Shane motioned north, toward Canada. "You hear what I'm saying?"

Carrie nodded. Minneapolis news was filled with drug runners and their deadly packages filtering into American cities. But that was on TV, not part of her world.

"Gichigami here is our friend." Shane stood, tipping his bottle toward the lake. "Her deep waters keep our secrets. So when someone threatens to tip off border agents, like that ol' boy, it's how we take care of business."

Carrie felt the air leave her lungs, imagining the concrete block tied to her own waist, the cold water rushing over her as the heavy rock pulled her down . . . . "You can go on with your *business.* I won't say a word!"

Streaks of amber sunlight filtered through the stained windowpanes. Nearby a robin sang. Carrie's emotions surged into a never before felt realization . . . the world would go on and no one would ever know what happened to her.

Shane paced behind her, his boots sounding a steady rhythm on the wooden floor. Carrie watched his reflection, duplicated in the shard pieces of an ornate mirror. Sully and Eddie waited, anticipating Shane's order.

"My girls *need* me," she whispered, fighting tears.

"This ain't easy." Shane's expression was serious, haunting. "I've never killed a woman."

The boot steps halted. Shane reached a hand to Carrie's face. "Rule Number One, no witnesses." He bent down, tracing a finger along her cheek. She felt his breath against her neck. "I'm sorry . . . ."

"*Please*, I'm begging."

Shane nodded to Sully and Eddie. The two moved toward her, eager to carry out their task.

"Wait!" Desperation channeled into adrenaline. "What if," Carrie said, her voice raspy, "there was a way to make it even? What if . . . we had to trust each other?"

Shane tilted his head. "Talk to me, pretty lady."

Carrie poured a cup of coffee for her sister and joined her in the living room. "It's so good to have you home," Sheila said. "The kids are having a ball together, aren't they?" The first snowfall had blanketed the plains of Nebraska in a chenille covering that glimmered like diamonds.

Standing at the picture window, the sisters watched the cousins play. Sheila lowered her voice, even though they were alone. "It's weird how Tony disappeared, isn't it? I mean, without a trace? What did those investigators say?"

"Nothing really." Carrie patted her sister's arm. "He probably ran off to the Caribbean. You know how he loves the water."

Broken Promises

His vow to love, honor and cherish—
drowned by spilled milk pails,
pecked by angry laying hens,
swatted by flying cow tails,
gagged by greasy gravy,
burned by broken promises.

My vow to love, honor and obey—
shattered dishes against the door,
stomped his laundry in mud puddles,
dumped dinner on the kitchen floor,
splattered eggs at our wedding picture,
ignited by broken promises.

With fire in his eyes he watched as I
packed my stained dresses and broke free,
away from the man who said I was lucky
to have him, poor country girl like me.
I sat in my car with no place to go, but
nowhere, anywhere was better than here.

Alone, I feel an empty happiness as I
see a world beyond fields of corn stubble,
hear music and laughter, not cows bawling,
touch my hands now smooth and supple,
smell fresh air with no hint of the barnyard,
taste food that isn't meat and potatoes.

I sift through ashes of broken promises and
remember our vows for better or for worse.
My sixth sense burns like a smoldering ember—
Had he broken our promise or had I?

Poetry - Sarah J. Cox

Stones

Terrazin (Teresianstadt) October 28, 2011

We walk on cobblestones to see these horrors.
It is fitting—after a time they hurt your feet.
But think of those feet that stumbled along these streets
weary from labor and starvation, heading for trains
to Auschwitz, Sobibor, Dachau. Stones.

These walls are built of stones,
walling off a people from their life,
from one another, husbands from wives,
brothers from sisters, parents from children,
fencing off the world that did not want to know
what lay within. Stones.

The graves are marked by stones, row upon row.
Rosebushes bloom feebly between each stone
in this October grey. One hundred thousand buried here,
perhaps a thousand markers. The rest,
nameless bones lifted from a mass grave
reburied beneath these stones. Stones.

Jews, remembering old desert practices,
leave pebbles on gravestones.
Here, on each weathered gravestone
a single pebble, or two, or a dozen,
plucked from the gravel path to honor a death.
The pebbles say, *Someone has passed this way.*
Someone remembers. Stones.

Once, on a New year's Eve, guards distracted
by drink and celebration, a few prisoners escaped
and got away. Others, not so fortunate,
were recaptured, returned. Their punishment?
The other prisoners were forced
to stone them to death. With stones. Stones.

For good, for evil. For building up, for tearing down.
For creating, for destroying.
For dreams, for the crushing of dreams,
For living, for dying. Stones.

Dear Military Service Member

I have a deep need to do two things: call you by a name (Sam, Margo, Mario, Tianyi) and picture you in a specific place (West Texas, North Carolina, Afghanistan). But I'm able to do neither. You are someone I don't know, someone in some where I have probably never been. But I feel the reality of your life just as sure as I feel these keys under my fingers, and it's a bit miraculous to understand that what I'm about to say will reach you, whatever letters it takes to make up your name.

Let me start here: I'm Emily. I live in Carver County, Minnesota. On the green couch where I write now, I have a view through the window of the night stretched before me, and it's an inky black liquid in the way the wind pushes it in all directions. The clouds hang low and thick, so no glimmers from stars or moon slip in. Tomorrow is the winter solstice, the shortest day of the year. Details like this always make me pause and wonder about tides and dormancy and long and short shadows and the other side of the world. I can't help looking for some significance.

In the morning, the light will sift through the clouds and lay thin fingers on our strange December. Last winter at this time, Minneapolis had had almost forty inches of snow, and I'd already taken frigid, awkward walks in too-big-for-me boots. But yesterday I still selected my autumn coat and chose my scarf by color, not warmth. There is no snow here, only brown grasses, still green in some places, that when walked on feel hard as stone. I wear small, thin shoes, and feel the earth tightening beneath me.

Do you know what I mean?

When the first real snow comes, it will cause traffic jams and spin-outs and missed meetings. Fingers will shrink with the cold, cheeks will pink at the wind's bite, and there will be cursing on every street. But I keep thinking that the white will also be widely welcomed, embraced even by those with long driveways, because of the wait. The wanting. The wonder over what has kept it away, all those reasons that are each little stories of other lives.

You know? On Friday, I will drive through county after county, up Interstate 94, past hundreds of acres of furrowed fields, dusty with dry soil, toward my parents' home. I will look for hearty birds. I will scout out signs of deer inside stands of grey woods. I will watch the sky shift above me, holding out handfuls of blue, and I will think of you. I will wonder where you are this Christmas. I'll imagine, if not your face, then your feet, the weight of your boots, the way they hit the ground, if that ground gives a little.

You are walking somewhere I don't know, perhaps somewhere that you haven't known yourself for very long. And really, it is miraculous, because in a way you are walking that path for me. For so many people who will never know if it snows outside your window or if there's heat, if you like one or both, what the night looks like to you when you stare into it, or the letters of your name.

The Immigrant, 1906

Stoically shook Father's hand,
awkwardly embraced Mother,
boarded the train bound for Helsinki
and the boat.
Seventeen, on his way to America,
never to return
or speak to his parents again.
Ship mail was slow, but they would write.

Minnesota held forests and lakes,
reminders of home.
Offered work on railroads
and lumber camps.
In his suitcase were some clothes,
a few photographs,
courage and determination.
He carried dreams by the handle.

Poetry - Sister Kate Martin

Still There

The tools are still at hand, their shapes, at least, the same as in the days when I rejoiced to use them, to feel the sharp edge of the word-blade and the hum of an inner rhythm fully engaged. The room looks the same: table, chair, paper and pen, door closed against unexpected company, window open to catch the possible breeze of inspiration. Some things are new, having slipped in when I wasn't looking: lethargy, with its moods and bulk, mumbling to me in monosyllables now and then, and loquacious fear, reciting the certainty that heart and hand and eye have lost the impulse of collaboration. Poetry is gone, says fear, and no pen of yours will call it up again.

And I, tempted to give in to such discouragements, would do so now if it were not for the web of branches just outside the window and its layer of shining frost, with the cold blue sky so exultant, and the red bravado of that cardinal whistling ecstatically into my ear, my eye, into the pencil in my hand.

Contributors

2011

We would like to thank our generous contributors for helping make this year's Talking Stick possible!

Friends/Single
Jodi Buchan
Sandy Freeman
Peggy Trojan
LuAnne L. White

Good Friends/Single
Richard Hagen
Rhoda Jackson
Sonja Kosler
Joanne Moren
Jim Russell

Friends/Couple
Patricia and Don Conner
Marion and John Holtey

Good Friends/Couple
Jere Truer

Special Friends/Single
Nona Kennedy Carlson
Laurie Fabrizio
Michael Lein
Anne Morgan
Shasha C. Porter
Candace Simar
Faith Sullivan

Special Friends/Couple
Ed & Genell Poitras

Benefactors
Marge Barrett
Louise Bottrell
Audrae Gruber
Kathryn Medellin
Niomi Rohn Phillips
Marlene and Harlan Stoehr

"The Talking Stick is a Native American tradition used to facilitate an orderly discussion. The stick is made of wood, decorated with feathers or fur, beads or paint, or a combination of all. Usually speakers are arranged in a talking circle and the stick is passed from hand to hand as the discussion progresses. It encourages all to speak and allows each person to speak without interruption. The Talking Stick brings all natural elements together to guide and direct the talking circle."

-Anne M. Dunn

This year, we received 278 submissions from 134 writers. The editorial board selected 94 poems, 22 creative nonfiction, and 14 fiction pieces from 95 writers for inclusion in this volume.
Please submit again!

Thank you for your support!
Visit us at:
www.thetalkingstick.com
www.jackpinewriters.com

Made in the USA
Charleston, SC
25 July 2012